The Anti-Capitalist Chronicles

Red Letter

The Anti-Capitalist Chronicles

David Harvey

Edited by Jordan T. Camp and Chris Caruso

PLUTO  PRESS

First published 2020 by Pluto Press
345 Archway Road, London N6 5AA

www.plutobooks.com

Copyright © David Harvey 2020

The right of David Harvey to be identified as the author of this work has been
asserted in accordance with the Copyright, Designs and Patents Act 1988.

British Library Cataloguing in Publication Data
A catalogue record for this book is available from the British Library

ISBN   978 0 7453 4208 5   Hardback
ISBN   978 0 7453 4209 2   Paperback
ISBN   978 1 7868 0774 8   PDF eBook
ISBN   978 1 7868 0776 2   Kindle eBook
ISBN   978 1 7868 0775 5   EPUB eBook

Typeset by Stanford DTP Services, Northampton, England

Simultaneously printed in the United Kingdom and United States of America

Contents

Preface

Jordan T. Camp

With *The Anti-Capitalist Chronicles*, my co-editors, Christina Heatherton and Manu Karuka, and I are immensely proud to launch our Red Letter book series. Red Letter features works by intellectuals invested in the struggles of the poor, working class, and dispossessed in North America from an internationalist perspective. Inspired by Antonio Gramsci, we publish works by emerging radical intellectuals, authors, scholars, and permanent persuaders of political and social movements. Amidst a surging interest in socialism, our books are intended as resources for popular education in working-class and socialist movements, as well as for classroom adoption. Our goal is to place anti-imperialism and class struggle at the heart of the political and intellectual agenda.

The Anti-Capitalist Chronicles was conceived as an intervention in debates around the crisis of neoliberal capitalism and the renewal of the socialist left. It was developed through discussions at The People's Forum, a movement incubator and educational and cultural space in New York City. In this endeavor we have been fortunate to interact with political and social movements across the United States and Global South including the Landless Workers' Movement (MST) in Brazil; South Africa's Abahlali baseMjondolo, the shack-dweller's movement and the National Union of Metalworkers South Africa (NUMSA); and the Poor People's Campaign, Fight for $15, anti-war movements in North America, and many more. In these struggles, we see new visions for fundamental social change arising. We are immensely proud to work in collaboration with some of the foremost Marxist scholars in the United States and in the world, namely, David Harvey.

Few possess the clarity and foresight of world-renowned Marxist theorist, David Harvey. Since the publication of his bestselling

A Brief History of Neoliberalism (2005), Harvey has been tracking the evolution of the neoliberal capitalism as well as tides of radical opposition rising against it. Now, amidst waves of economic crisis, class struggle, and neo-fascist reaction, Harvey defines how socialist alternatives to capitalism are possible, and elucidates how the transition to socialism can and must be organized by the movements. *The Anti-Capitalist Chronicles* represents Harvey's reflections on crisis and possibility, an update and clear-eyed assessment of the intervening years since *A Brief History of Neoliberalism* was first published.

While some works declare neoliberalism dead, *The Anti-Capitalist Chronicles* contends that the neoliberal project is very much alive, but, significantly, with its legitimacy lost. Neoliberalism, unable to command the consent it once did, has developed alliances with neo-fascism in order to survive. The rise of nationalist and violent reactionary forces is therefore not ancillary or accidental to the survival of capitalism; as Harvey argues, such violence has been present since its bloody inception.[1] In *A Brief History*, Harvey argued that the CIA-backed coup in Chile in 1973 marked a critical moment in the turn to neoliberalism. At the time, US President Richard Nixon ordered the CIA to "make the economy scream" in Chile in order to prevent democratically elected socialist, Salvador Allende "from coming to power." Democratic forces were violently repressed by military force. In our present moment of US-backed coups in Latin America, US support for the far right, and the repression of left political movements in the hemisphere, Harvey's insights are critical to understand the evolution of the neoliberal state, and indeed, the struggle before us.[2]

Then, as now, the rise of the neoliberal state is inconceivable outside of class struggles across the US and the world. In the 1960s

---

1. Jipson John and Jitheesh P.M., "'The Neoliberal Project is Alive but Has Lost its Legitimacy': An Interview with David Harvey," *The Wire*, February 16, 2019, https://thewire.in/economy/david-harvey-marxist-scholar-neo-liberalism (accessed May 12, 2020).
2. Nixon quoted in Peter Kornbluh, "Chile and the United States: Declassified Documents Relating to the Military Coup, September 11, 1973," National Security Archive Electronic Briefing Book no. 8, https://nsarchive2.gwu.edu//NSAEBB/NSAEBB8/nsaebb8i.htm (accessed May 12, 2020); David Harvey, *A Brief History of Neoliberalism* (Oxford: Oxford University Press, 2005), 7–9.

and 1970s, national liberation and socialist struggles circulated across Africa, Asia, and Latin America. These struggles were linked to an expanding geography of urban insurgencies in North America and Europe. Anti-imperialist struggles in places like Vietnam, as I have argued, were concretely linked to uprisings in places like Watts in 1965 and Detroit in 1967. Taken together, these struggles led to a crisis of hegemony for capital and the state. The political response of state and capitalist forces to this crisis produced a new historical and geographical conjuncture. The rise of neoliberalism cannot be understood outside of this global context of insurgency.[3]

In this period, as *A Brief History of Neoliberalism* describes, the interests of the ruling class were shown to be disconnected from the interests of the masses. Increased expenditures on warfare and militarism, such as mass incarceration and policing, contributed to neoliberalism's legitimacy crisis. In order to resolve this crisis, capitalist states promoted authoritarian politics and free market solutions. It is from these efforts that we can mark the neoliberal turn. This global neoliberal counterrevolution, we should remember, was the product of political and class struggles; ones that could have had, and that still could have, different outcomes.[4]

The development of the neoliberal state has been accompanied by the production of a historically specific common sense. Harvey employs the concept of common sense as Italian Marxist theorist Antonio Gramsci did, to describe the "generally held assumptions and beliefs" that secure consent to coercion.[5] Common sense

3. David Harvey, *The Limits to Capital* (New York: Verso, 2006), x–xi; Vijay Prashad, *The Poorer Nations: A Possible History of the Global South* (New York: Verso, 2012), 5; Jordan T. Camp, *Incarcerating the Crisis: Freedom Struggles and the Rise of the Neoliberal State* (Oakland: University of California Press, 2016); Neil Smith, *Uneven Development: Nature, Capital, and the Production of Space* (Athens: University of Georgia Press, 2010), 240.
4. Giovanni Arrighi, *Adam Smith in Beijing: Lineages of the 21st Century* (New York: Verso, 2007), 154–5; Ruth Wilson Gilmore, *Golden Gulag: Prisons, Surplus, and Opposition in Globalizing California* (Berkeley: University of California Press, 2007); Jordan T. Camp, "The Bombs Explode at Home: Policing, Prisons, and Permanent War," *Social Justice* 44, no. 2–3 (2017): 21; Gillian Hart, "D/developments after the Meltdown," *Antipode* 41, no. S1 (2009): 117–41; Camp, *Incarcerating the Crisis*.
5. Antonio Gramsci, *Selections from the Prison Notebooks* (New York: International Publishers, 2003 [1971]), 323, 328.

obscures the sources of political and economic problems through culturalist and nationalist narratives about race, gender, sexuality, religion, the family, freedom, corruption, and law and order. These narratives have been mobilized to secure consent to what Harvey describes as the "restoration of class power." Harvey argues that political questions are difficult to answer when they are concealed as cultural narratives. Hurricane Katrina in New Orleans in 2005, for instance, represented an environmental catastrophe that required state organized evacuation plans, the deployment of emergency public health measures, and the distribution of food and medicine. This catastrophe was recast as a racist crisis of law and order, one resolved by the state through police, military intervention, and guns. Such a redefinition enabled federal funds to be diverted into repression and corporate investments rather than towards survival, a clear project of class restoration.[6]

Neoliberal common sense has circulated for decades through the media, universities, and think tanks. In opposition to it, anti-capitalist movements across Africa, Asia, the Americas, and Europe have drawn on Harvey's theoretical work to counter its circulation. These mass movements of the left, as well as cycles of protests against austerity from Chile to Lebanon to Haiti, reveal that neoliberalism is no longer able to secure the consent of the masses. The current state of affairs represents what Gramsci referred to as a "crisis of authority" or a moment where the "ruling class has lost its consensus," i.e. is "no longer 'leading' but only 'dominant', exercising coercive force alone," and therefore "this means that the great masses have become detached from the traditional ideologies, and no longer believe what they used to." Such a moment is unpredictable, but it offers a unique opportunity for activists and forces of opposition to organize.[7]

---

6. Harvey, *A Brief History of Neoliberalism*, 39; Clyde Woods, *Development Drowned and Reborn: The Blues and Bourbon Restorations in Post-Katrina New Orleans*, ed. Jordan T. Camp and Laura Pulido (Athens: University of Georgia Press, 2017).
7. Gramsci, *Selections from the Prison Notebooks*, 275–6; Jordan T. Camp and Jennifer Greenburg, "Counterinsurgency Reexamined: Racism, Capitalism, and U.S. Military Doctrine," *Antipode* 52 no. 2 (2020): 430–51.

While the neoliberal state's legitimacy has eroded, *The Anti-Capitalist Chronicles* argues that its political project is *alive and well*. To update his analysis of *A Brief History* for the present moment, Harvey proposes that neoliberalism cannot presently survive without an alliance with neo-fascism. To sustain this argument, he explores how the far-right President Jair Bolsonaro's administration in Brazil has used violence and racist, sexist, and reactionary common sense appeals to impose a neoliberal model. He draws out the similarities with Augusto Pinochet's regime in Chile after the CIA-backed coup installed him in 1973. Over the course of his political career, Bolsonaro has praised the military dictatorship which ruled Brazil in the 1970s and 1980s. He publicly extolled the man who had tortured former Brazilian president Dilma Rouseff under the dictatorship, herself impeached in a "parliamentary coup" in 2016. Bolsonaro has exploited anxieties about drugs, gangs, and crime in the favelas to win consent to a neo-fascist project, which combines a commitment to crush the socialist left with an attack on democracy. As Harvey suggests, Bolsonaro exploits common sense narratives to restore class power in the country and region.[8]

The rise of Bolsonaro is a political expression of the crisis of capitalism and of the neoliberal state; a crisis in which the system is not able to go on in the way that it has. The crisis, as economist and cofounder of the Landless Workers' Movement (MST) in Brazil, João Pedro Stedile argues, is "characterized by calling into question the essence of the capitalist mode of production, now hegemonized by financial capital and the large international corporations" that controls global production. The current crisis, according to Stedile, painfully exposes how capitalism is unable to resolve its inherent contradictions. Capital, in other words, cannot enable the unfettered accumulation of wealth while also meeting the needs of the impov-

---

8. Vincent Bevins, "The Dirty Problems with Operation Carwash," *The Atlantic*, August 21, 2019, www.theatlantic.com/international/archive/2019/08/anti-corruption-crusades-paved-way-bolsonaro/596449/ (accessed May 12, 2020); The Intercept, Secret Brazil Archive, https://theintercept.com/series/secret-brazil-archive/ (accessed May 12, 2020); Jordan T. Camp, "The Rise of the Right in Latin America: An Interview with Stephanie Weatherbee Brito," The New Intellectuals, March 12, 2020, https://tpf.link/tni (accessed June 15, 2020).

erished majority; it has no program for the people or for the country. The Bolsonaro government represents an uneasy alliance between the financiers of the Chicago School, Evangelical Christian fundamentalists, and the most conservative sectors of the military. They promote so-called free market solutions to problems backed with the full weight of state repression and the criminalization of protest. Neoliberals in Bolsonaro's Brazil, Stedile argues, actively promote the policies premiered by the Chilean dictatorship, just in a new context. Significantly, the current far-right Brazilian government is supported by the Trump administration, which is actively pursuing an openly aggressive imperial strategy in Latin America.[9]

In 2010 Harvey delivered a lecture, "Organizing for the Anti-Capitalist Transition" at the World Social Forum in Porto Alegre, Brazil. He argued that the hegemonic crisis that took shape after the 2007–08 global financial crisis represented an opportunity to build a truly global anti-capitalist movement. He suggested that Lenin's question "what is to be done?" could not be fully answered without the formation of political organizations capable of seizing state power and articulating alternative solutions to "perpetual future crises of capitalism with increasingly deadly results." He concluded that "Lenin's question demands an answer."[10]

To answer that question at present, Harvey advocates building anti-capitalist movements with the strategic goal of controlling "both production and the distribution of surpluses." As struggles become radicalized, understanding the source of their problems as systemic and structural, "rather than particular and local," the germ of this movement becomes evident. It is upon this terrain, Harvey argues, that "the figure of the 'organic intellectual' leader, made so much of in Antonio Gramsci's work, the autodidact who comes to understand the world first hand through bitter experiences, but

9. João Pedro Stedile, "Contemporary Challenges for the Working Class and Peasantry in Brazil," *Monthly Review*, July 1, 2019, https://monthlyreview.org/2019/07/01/contemporary-challenges-for-the-working-class-and-peasantry-in-brazil/ (accessed May 12, 2020).

10. David Harvey, "Organizing for the Anti-Capitalist Transition," talk at the 2010 World Social Forum, Porto Alegre, Brazil, http://davidharvey.org/2009/12/organizing-for-the-anti-capitalist-transition/ (accessed May 12, 2020).

shapes his or her understanding of capitalism more generally, has a great deal to say." In this regard, Harvey suggests that it is imperative to learn to listen to the organic intellectuals of political and social movements in Brazil, India, and across the Global South. "In this instance," Harvey writes, "the task … is to magnify the subaltern voice so that attention can be paid to the circumstances of exploitation and repression and the answers that can be shaped into an anti-capitalist program."[11]

The Anti-Capitalist Chronicles is part of this larger effort to shape an anti-capitalist program. It does so amidst an illustrative moment of neoliberalism's depravity. At the time of this writing, the current coronavirus global pandemic is ravaging the United States and the world. While people in the United States are in desperate need of medical care, emergency protective supplies, and federal funds to pay rent, buy food, and stay alive, the crisis is being redefined through racist and nationalist narratives by the Trump administration. Instead of investing in life, his administration is advocating that people go back to work for the good of the country and that federal money be diverted not to emergency medical interventions, but to banks and corporations. With The Anti-Capitalist Chronicles, Harvey helps activists "extract political meanings" from these diverting cultural constructions.[12] By highlighting the causes and consequences of the current crisis, Harvey shows that there is "no such thing as a truly natural disaster." Indeed, as he argues, the last four decades of neoliberal policies have left the public "totally exposed and ill-prepared to face a public health crisis of this sort." Survival will depend on overcoming these conditions.[13]

At this present moment, the irrationality of neoliberal solutions to crisis are rendered more vivid than ever. Ideologues of the far right are advocating that the poor, the ill, and the elderly sacrifice their lives by going to work for the so-called good of "the nation." It is clear that capital cannot pursue free market solutions to the crisis

---

11. Ibid.
12. Harvey, *A Brief History of Neoliberalism*, 39.
13. Harvey, "Anti-Capitalist Politics in a Time of COVID-19," chapter 18, this volume.

and simultaneously meet the needs of the impoverished majority. The poor, the working class, and the dispossessed have been essentially rendered disposable even while their labor is recognized as essential. "Unemployment levels will almost certainly rise to levels comparable to the 1930s," Harvey warns, "in the absence of state interventions that will have to go against the neoliberal grain." This situation undoubtedly represents a crisis. As Harvey shows, it also presents an unprecedented opportunity to brush against the grain. Such an effort will require popular education and political mobilization to illustrate the possibilities of a socialist alternative. This, as Harvey shows us, is the anti-capitalist imperative of our time. We hope this book will assist all those engaged in this struggle.[14]

---

14. Ibid; *New Frame* Editorial, "Coronavirus and the Crisis of Capitalism," *New Frame*, March 13, 2020, www.newframe.com/coronavirus-and-the-crisis-of-capitalism/ (accessed May 12, 2020).

Editors' Note

Jordan T. Camp and Chris Caruso

In this book, *The Anti-Capitalist Chronicles*, David Harvey, leading Marxist geographer and theorist of capitalism, offers interventions in the current conjuncture. It provides timely observations and incisive interventions into current events and contemporary debates. Likewise, the book offers a Marxist framework for analyzing the underappreciated features of anti-capitalist struggles and their connections internationally.

Few are better situated to discuss the present crisis of capitalism and the crossroads of political possibility. A leading theorist in the field of urban studies whom *Library Journal* called "one of the most influential geographers of the later twentieth century," David Harvey is Distinguished Professor of Anthropology and Earth and Environmental Sciences at the Graduate Center of the City University of New York and author of more than twenty books.

Harvey speaks internationally not just on campuses and institutes but also in homeless encampments, takeover buildings, popular education schools, prisons, activist gatherings, and more. He is a public intellectual in dialogue with dozens of social movements around the globe. David Harvey earned his PhD from Cambridge University and was formerly professor of geography at Johns Hopkins, a Miliband Fellow at the London School of Economics, and Halford Mackinder Professor of Geography at Oxford.

While noted as one of the most cited authors in the humanities and social sciences, since the publication of *The New Imperialism* (2003), Harvey has been increasingly focused on writing for a popular audience, in books including *A Brief History of Neoliberalism* (2005), *The Enigma of Capital* (2010), *Seventeen Contradictions and the End of Capitalism* (2014), and *Marx, Capital, and the Madness of Economic Reason* (2017).

Alongside these publications, Harvey has also been an innovator in the online space for over a decade. Harvey has more than 120,000 followers on Twitter (@profdavidharvey) and a very active website (davidharvey.org) and social media presence. Senior demographer at the Pew Research Center, Conrad Hackett, posted a list of most followed sociologists on Twitter in 2017, and David Harvey ranked number four. Hackett also linked to a list of the top economists on Twitter, by followers, and Harvey ranked number 15. This is a testament to Harvey's broad influence that he was the only person to appear on both lists, even though neither a sociologist nor an economist.

The book is inspired by Harvey's *Anti-Capitalist Chronicles*, a bi-monthly podcast and online video series that looks at contemporary capitalism through a Marxist lens. The podcast is made possible by Democracy at Work, a non-profit that produces media and live events. Their work analyzes capitalism as a systemic problem and advocates systemic solutions. This is not the first book of David Harvey's inspired by his online digital projects. In 2008, David Harvey and co-editor Chris Caruso produced "Reading Marx's *Capital* with David Harvey," a free online video course (http://davidharvey.org/reading-capital/). Harvey's online courses and accompanying website attracted a large global audience and were viewed over four and a half million times in over two hundred countries. That audience took action in various ways including the self-organization of hundreds of *Capital* study circles around the globe and the spontaneous crowd-sourced initiative which is translating Professor Harvey's Volume 1 lectures into 45 languages.

The viral success of the *Capital* classes has been credited with reviving an interest in studying Marx which had waned since the fall of the Berlin Wall in 1989. The "Reading Marx's *Capital*" online course presaged the later development of the Massively Open Online Course (MOOC) and represented innovation in educational technology that is now widely emulated. Those online classes were the inspiration for *A Companion to Marx's Capital* (2010) and *A Companion to Marx's Capital, Volume 2* (2013).

The analysis put forth in *The Anti-Capitalist Chronicles* is essential for political and social movements and everyday people concerned about injustice in mapping the current terrain of class struggle. Written in a conversational style, we see this volume offering a new, accessible entry point into his larger body of work. It is suitable for those reading David Harvey for the first time as well as those who are well versed in his writings. At the end of the book, we have provided both recommendations for further reading on the topic as well as discussion questions for each chapter. Based on the global phenomenon of study circles spontaneously arising around the "Reading Marx's *Capital* with David Harvey" course, we have structured this book to be used as a tool for popular education for organizers, activists, and others, as well as more formal classroom settings.

Throughout the 19 chapters, Harvey treats contemporary issues including the concentration of finance and monetary power in the economy, the COVID-19 pandemic, the General Motors plant closing, the emerging alliance between neoliberals and neo-fascists in Brazil and across the globe, the significance of China in the global economy, and carbon dioxide emissions and climate change. He takes up key concepts in Marxism and socialism including the origins and development of capital, alienation, socialism and "un-freedom," and the geography and geopolitics of capital accumulation. Harvey considers the attempts and failures of the Trump administration to solve the crisis of neoliberalism, and the necessity of organizing a socialist alternative.

These are dark and dangerous days where there is great need for deep analysis and understanding of the forces arrayed against us as well as visionary alternatives for transforming society to meet the needs of all. Harvey's work has contributed to the renewal of the Marxist tradition which has served as a beacon for revolutionaries for over a century. This book offers a rekindling of that tradition to light our way as we face the urgent life and death struggles of our time.

Author's Note

David Harvey

The idea for the podcasts that came to be called *The Anti-Capitalist Chronicles* arose out of discussions with the Democracy at Work media initiative in November 2018. I thank Rick Wolff for setting the idea in motion as well as providing the necessary infrastructure for putting the podcasts online. I also thank Maria Carnemolla Mania for managing the series along with Bryan Isom for his tireless commitment to recording and putting the podcasts into broadcast mode. I was somewhat surprised later at the proposal by Jordan Camp and Chris Caruso to create a publishable version of the Chronicles, through the medium of Pluto Press. I was not entirely convinced it was a good idea but am now persuaded of its utility, if only for pedagogic purposes, given the current challenging political circumstances. I have been delighted in any case to support the initiatives of the newly founded People's Forum in New York by shifting some of my teaching obligations as well as my library into the public sphere with the Forum's help. I am pleased to help launch Red Letter. I had no overall plan in mind in approaching the podcasts. I relied upon current events and the evolution of my own interests along with those of close colleagues and friends to dictate the flow of ideas. While the result may appear somewhat chaotic, some astute editing by Jordan and Chris, along with suggestions from the editorial group have helped give shape to the project. Finally, I have appreciated all the help I have had over the years from Chris Caruso, in bringing the Marxist perspective of the totality into the mainstream of anti-capitalist strategizing. The times are dangerous but also opportune for the exploration of new possibilities.

Acknowledgements

We are grateful to The People's Forum for supporting this project, and particularly to Claudia de la Cruz, Manolo de los Santos, Layan Fuleihan, David Chung, Belén Marco Crespo, Bryant Diaz, Juan Peralta, Rita Henderson, and many others. Working with acquisitions editor David Shulman has been a pleasure. We want to thank him and his colleagues David Castle and Veruschka Selbach at Pluto Press for the encouragement and support of Red Letter. Robert Webb guided us through the production process. Many thanks to Aya Ouais for research assistance and transcriptions for this book, Elaine Ross for the copy edits, and Melanie Patrick for the cover design. Our deepest thanks to Christina Heatherton, Manu Karuka, Kanishka Goonewardena, and the Racial Capitalism Working Group in the Center for the Study of Social Difference at Columbia University for invaluable workshop feedback leading to this publication.

Jordan T. Camp would like to thank the Center for Place, Culture and Politics at the Graduate Center of the City University of New York for offering vital and generative intellectual community to complete the book as a visiting scholar. Conversations with Ruth Wilson Gilmore, David Harvey, Peter Hitchcock, Zifeng Liu, Maria Luisa Mendonca, Lou Cornom, Mary Taylor, and many more have nourished the editing process.

Chris Caruso would like to thank David Harvey for his generosity in pursuing this book project, his support of social movement initiatives around the world, and our now 15-year collaboration in online political education. Thanks also to comrades and mentors Willie Baptist, Roy Singham, General Baker, Marian Kramer, Kathleen Sullivan, and Ronald Casanova for their insistence on the necessity of rigorous political education towards the development of organic intellectuals from the ranks of the poor and the dispossessed. Gratitude to my wife Liz and children Sophia and Luke for their hope and inspiration.

1
Global Unrest

The huge outburst of political struggles around the world in the fall of 2019 – from Santiago to Beirut, Baghdad, Tehran, Paris, Quito, Hong Kong, India, Algeria, Sudan and well beyond – suggests that there is something chronically wrong in the world. In part the problems can be traced to failings in democratic governance and a general alienation from dominant political practices. The other familiar complaint is the failure of the dominant economic model that is supposed to keep us employed at adequate incomes, put affordable food upon our table, shirts on our backs, shoes on our feet, phones in our hands and autos in our garages, while delivering a range of those collective services (healthcare, education, housing, and transportation) to guarantee a reasonably satisfying quality of daily life.

Recent events in Chile appear to be emblematic not only with respect to the nature of the problems but also to the typical means by which they get politically addressed. I have long followed Chile because it was one of the initiators of the neoliberal turn back in 1973 when General Pinochet dislodged Salvador Allende, the dem-ocratically elected socialist president, in a military coup, and installed the "Chicago Boys" economists who imposed the neoliberal economic model on the country. In an interview with the *Financial Times* in early October 2019, President Piñera, a conservative business man, depicted Chile as an "oasis" of sound growth, a strong economy, and excellent economic indicators. Chile, he asserted, was in excellent shape, a model for the rest of Latin America. About three weeks after, news flashes reported a serious uprising underway in Chile. The initial problem was an increase in subway fares. High school students took to the streets (much as they had done in 2006) in protest. Piñera, from the comfort of an upscale restaurant, vowed to curb the lawless rabble of trouble-makers. This was a tacit invitation to the police to go out and violently quell the discontent. The police obliged. Many more people joined the protests against the police. Some subway stations were burned down along with three churches. Supermarkets were attacked. A state of emergency was declared. The military were called upon and soon millions of outraged citizens were peacefully protesting everything, including the presence of the military (who had not been seen on the streets since the years of the dictatorship). Piñera belatedly recognized that he needed to listen and do something. He increased pensions and social security and raised the minimum wage. He called off the state of emergency and asked the security forces to back off. The demand arose that Chile needed a new constitution. The existing neoliberal one was drawn up during the military dictatorship. It mandated the privatization of pensions, health, education, and the like. It was ultimately agreed that the constitution was in need of revision. A plebiscite on how to do it was proposed for April 2020 (most recently postponed because of the coronavirus). An uneasy peace descended on the land.

Events in Chile were not isolated. Something similar had earlier happened in Ecuador. The International Monetary Fund (IMF) had mandated structural adjustment and that meant new taxes and the abolition of fuel subsidies. This provoked mass protests. Indigenous populations had already been in motion, and marched en masse upon Quito, the capital city (with echoes of the 1990s and the protests that had earlier brought the socialist Rafael Correa to power). The protests threatened to be so large that the government decamped to Guayaquil, leaving Quito in the hands of protestors. Eventually President Moreno – whose first name is Lenin – annulled the IMF program and returned to Quito to negotiate.

Chile and Ecuador were in turmoil in the fall of 2019. In a very different direction, Bolivia was also troubled. Evo Morales, the president, was accused by powerful forces on the right wing, backed by organized street demonstrations, of manipulating the election results in his favor. At the "insistence" of the military, he and his government officials fled the country to seek asylum elsewhere. Mass movements were on the streets and conflicting groups clashed with each other. Bolivia is in turmoil pending new elections in June (now postponed), though Morales is banned from running (much as Lula was in Brazil prior to Bolsonaro's election).

Across the other side of the world, Lebanon was also in turmoil. Frustrated youth have repeatedly taken to the streets in a mass movement of protest against the government. The same thing has been happening in Baghdad, in Iraq, but in this case two or three hundred people have been killed in mass demonstrations, which were mainly coming out of the low-income, impoverished areas of Baghdad that had been neglected politically for years. Something analogous has also been going on in Tehran. In France, the Gilets Jaunes protests have been going on (though with diminishing intensity) for a year or more, most recently intermingling with anti-government protests against pension reforms which closed down Paris and other major cities for a few days.

Civic protests are going on all over the place. If, from a spaceship way above planet Earth, we could see all places of protest flashing red, then we would almost certainly conclude that the world is in total turmoil. A wave of labor protests has also crested. In the United States, for example, teachers' strikes (many unofficial) have proliferated in recent years in the least likely of places, culminating in Chicago in September 2019. There have been some major strikes occurring in Bangladesh and India and also some major labor movements (though hard to trace or track) in China.

So what are all these protests about, do they have anything in common? In each instance, there are a range of particular concerns. The common thread seems to be the realization that the economy is not delivering on its promises for the masses of people and that the political process is warped in favor of the ultra-rich. It might be working for the top 1 percent, the top 10 percent, but it is not working for the masses and the masses are becoming conscious of this fact and are taking to the streets and protesting and saying this political-economic model is not responding to our basic needs.

In Chile, the top 1 percent controls about one-third of the wealth. The same problem arises almost everywhere. Increasing inequality seems to be at the root of the problems, and therefore it is not only the lower classes, but the middle classes who are suffering a great deal. What is it about the economy that is not working? In two or three of the cases, in fact, in Tehran, in Ecuador, and in Chile, there was a similar trigger for the uprising: an increase in fuel prices and transportation costs. For most people, getting around in the city is critical, and the cost of getting around is critical. If the cost becomes prohibitive, then low-income populations in particular are very hard hit. Hence, the sensitivity to increases in transport and fuel costs.

The interesting thing is how the trigger evolves to become generalized and systemic. Protests may have initially been based on transport and food prices, and in some instances also to lack of access to urban services and to adequate affordable housing. This typically constitutes the initial economic basis. But the protests rarely stay on that point. They proliferate and get generalized very quickly. There are two ways to think about this. The first is to attribute the problems to the particular form of capital accumulation, such as neoliberalism. The problem is not capitalism but its neoliberal form. There are even those in corporate sectors that may agree and contemplate reforms. In recent times, some business groups have recognized that they have focused far too much on efficiency and profitability, and that it is now important to address the social and environmental consequences of their actions. This says that the neoliberal model has brought us this far, but we've had enough of it and that we ought to go to a broader based version of what capital accumulation is all about. We need a more socially responsible and more equitable form of "conscience capitalism" it is said. And one of the general themes in the protests is against the increasing social inequality and that also needs to be addressed, it is conceded. The neoliberal form of capital is the problem.

In Chile, that argument is very explicit, because to the degree that the protests and the violence subsided, it was due to the president and the Congress collectively deciding they would have a referendum on the question of how they might best design a new constitution to replace the neoliberal one.

While there are some acute problems with the neoliberal form of capitalism that cry out for rectification, I do not agree that neoliberalism is the key problem. To begin with, there are some parts of the world where neoliberal capitalism is not dominant and the economic model is not working for the mass of the people there either. The problem is, in short, capitalism and not its particular neoliberal model. We are, I think, now becoming aware and conscious of the fact that this may well be the underlying problem.

The current wave of protests exhibits very little that is new. Over the last 30 years, we have witnessed multiple protest movements, many of which have focused on the deteriorating qualities of daily life, particularly though not exclusively in urban areas. While there have been labor protests as well, it is clear that most of the truly mass movements have been urban based and that they have evolved according to a different logic and been animated by a different class and social composition compared to the proletarian and working-class struggles that have traditionally anchored anti-capitalist struggles and anti-capitalist theorizing.

For example, in 2013, in Turkey, there was a protest against a proposal to replace Gezi Park in the center of Istanbul with a shopping mall. An all-too frequent sequence of events unfolded. The police, at the behest of President Erdogan, violently attacked the protesters. More people came out to protest the police violence. Before you knew it, there were mass protests not only in Istanbul, but in all of the other major cities in Turkey. A prolonged period of major nationwide protest ensued protesting the lack of public consultation or of democratic governance with effects persisting to the present.

The same thing happened a few weeks later in Brazil. A rise in bus fares sparked street protests by students in São Paulo. The police at the behest of the Governor of that State (rather than the mayor of São Paulo) were unleashed to violently crush the student protest movement, which immediately resulted in a widespread popular defense (some of it organized by the Black Block Anarchists) of the students. Pretty soon, protests spread like wildfire through about a hundred odd cities in Brazil. In Rio, huge protests continued for days and nights. The protests went far beyond issues of transportation. Public anger at the vast amount of money being spent on building new stadiums and infrastructures for the World Cup and the Olympic Games and the corruptions involved brought out massive numbers of protestors. It's not as if people don't appreciate soccer in Brazil, but what they don't appreciate is the way that so much money was being spent on these infrastructures, when there was no money for hospitals, and schools, and all of the things needed to improve the qualities of daily life.

There has been a long history now of similar mass mobilizations. These mass mobilizations generally don't last that long. Most of the mobilizations occur without warning, then they quiet down, and people forget about them, and then they erupt again. Over the last 30 years the number of mass mobilizations occurring again and again has escalated. Maybe it started back in the anti-globalization movement, when the World Trade Organization (WTO) meetings in Seattle were disrupted. Suddenly and unexpectedly, as far as the authorities were concerned, all kinds of people descended upon Seattle and protested. The delegates of the WTO conference couldn't get to the meetings. Then after that there was a whole period when every G20, or G8, or IMF, or World Bank meeting was picketed by large numbers of protestors. And then came Occupy Wall Street, and all manner of copy-cat movements around the world in 2011. We've seen again and again mass movements of these various kinds and in most instances they have sparked contagion effects. Protests in one part of the world animate protests in a completely different part of the world.

But none of these protests have persisted even as they periodically return. They have also often been very fragmented. Different groups participate in these mass mobilizations but rarely coordinate together even though they all belong on the same street. But this is maybe now changing. In Lebanon, for example, there has been a long and bitter history of conflict and civil war, which was largely waged by religious factions and religious groups against each other. But now

(2019), for the first time in many, many years, all of the religious factions came together (particularly the young people who lacked any economic prospects) and started to protest against the klepto-cratic, autocratic, oligarchic form of governance that was existing there and the total lack of economic opportunities particularly for the young people. In other words, everybody agreed, no matter what their religious faction, that the political-economic model was not working and there needed to be something radically different, and that something different had to be worked out between the different religious factions. For the first time ever, different oppositional factions got together and engaged in some mutual dialogue to protest the political-economic model and to demand the creation of some alternative (though what exactly remained obscure).

I experienced something of this sort first hand in Brazil, after Bol-sonaro was elected. He is heading up a very right-wing, authoritarian and evangelical Christian government albeit committed to neoliber-alization. There are in Brazil several left parties in opposition. There is the Workers' Party which is the big one and which formerly held power. But there are several fragmented left parties which have some political representation. Each political party has its own state-funded think tank. If you have representation in parliament, you get some money to set up a think tank to do policy research. There are six political parties of the left and they have not been in good commu-nication with each other in the past. In fact, they have often been violently opposed to each other. But when I visited there in the spring of 2019, all six parties had collectively got together to stage a week-long reflection on the political situation. At the end of the week, there was a joint mass rally in which all the political leaders came together. All of them gave talks together, hugged each other on the stage, and suddenly the vision is of a left that might all work together in a way which had not been seen before. It is the same, I gather, in Chile. Different left factions have actually got together and started to talk together about the prospect of creating a new constitution.

So maybe the right-wing lurch in politics around the world is inspiring a more collaborative ethos on the left. Maybe something is different this time. Perhaps the recent mobilizations can be institutionalized and organized to have staying power. There is a huge difference between mobilization and organization. Over the last 30 years we have witnessed an astonishing capacity to mobilize almost instantaneously thanks in part, of course, to social media. Even in the United States we have seen massive women's marches, immigrant rights protests, Black Lives Matter, "Me-Too," and so on. The mobilization has been spectacular. But long-term organization seems to be lacking. What we now see is perhaps the beginnings of the coming together of all those who feel that there is something wrong with the basic economic model; which needs to be radically changed in such a way as to provide health, and well-being, and good education, and good pension rights, and all the rest of it, to the mass of the population, rather than delivering strong economic growth, and strong economic benefits for the top 1 percent or the top 10 percent.

I have been trying to think through what this might mean: is there a central contradiction in the way in which capital is working these days which really needs to be addressed, and if so, what would that central contradiction be? An obvious serious problem is the level of social inequality. Almost every country in the world has experienced an increase of social inequality over the last 30 years. A lot of people feel it has gone too far, and therefore there has to be some sort of movement to try to recapture a much greater level of equality in society, that better public goods and services have to be delivered to the masses of the population. That is one question.

The second question is the problem of climate change and environmental degradation more generally. We know that climate change has reached a point where there has to be some sort of collective response. This is becoming clearer to more and more people around the world. The graph of carbon dioxide levels in the atmosphere over the last 800,000 years provided by the National Oceanic and Atmospheric Administration in the United States has been widely distributed and its political implications much discussed. There are serious and seemingly intractable problems of social inequality and environmental degradation. But there are also other reasons for considering capital as not only increasingly unreasonable and unfair in its evolutionary trajectory, but barbaric and even suicidal. If this is so, then plainly capital needs to be replaced by another economic order. In exactly the same way that Marx was outraged by the factory conditions that then prevailed in Britain (as revealed by Engels and the factory inspectors' reports), considering them as inhumane and totally unacceptable, so we can look at the current factory conditions in Bangladesh, or in China, and conclude "this is no way in which a civilized world should organize its production." But why does capital continue to organize production in this way when the technology exists to do otherwise?

And then there is an additional factor right now, one which Marx did not deal with but which has now become critical. Capital is always about growth: it has to be because it's animated by the pursuit of profit. A healthy capitalist economy is one where everybody has positive profits, which means that there is more value at the end of the day than there was at the beginning. The surplus value at the end of the day is then used, under the force of the "coercive laws" of competition, to create more value. Capitalist growth is compound growth. Compound growth is now the problem. The size of the global economy doubles about every 25 years.

In Marx's time, the doubling of the size of the economy in 25 years didn't really pose a problem. But that is not the case anymore. The $4 trillion economy that existed in 1950 grew to a $40 trillion economy as of 2000, and to an $80 trillion economy now (in constant 1990 dollars). If this continues, as the laws of motion of capital suggest it must, then we have to face a $160 trillion economy by 2050, $320 trillion by 2075, and $640 trillion at the end of the century. This is what compound growth does. It challenges all barriers and limits even as it seems in itself to postulate an impossibility of achieving its endless spiral of growth.

Marx cited Richard Price who, back in 1772, wrote a tract about compound interest. Price calculated that if you invested one penny on the date of the birth of Jesus Christ, at 5 percent compound interest, by the time you get to 1772, you would need 150 spheres the size of planet Earth, all solid gold, to match the value of the investment. If the penny was invested at simple interest, then by 1772 it would be worth only seven shillings and small change. Marx was emphatic about the impossibility of long-run compound interest. But the abstract laws of motion of capital entail the endless accumulation of capital without limit. The potentiality for this compounding growth to hit insurmountable limits was not a visible problem when Marx was writing. He possibly thought it unimaginable that capital would survive this long anyway. The exponential growth of the global money supply and of global credit moneys since 1970 testify to the underlying compounding growth trajectory and the critical problems posed for production, distribution, consumption and the realization of value within global markets under the rule of capital. Capital is having real difficulties finding profitable investment opportunities for the $80 trillion now available (much of it locked up in investment funds). And when it does, it has to subject as much labor as possible to the highest possible levels of exploitation in order to validate the wholesale creation of exchange value in created money forms. Where and how money capital can be profitably invested is a critical problem, particularly since there is only one kind of capital that can accumulate without limit, and that is money capital. The prospect of using the huge mass of investment moneys to address the two key questions of environmental degradation and social inequality without the interventions of a world government or at least strong coordination amongst the world's disparate governments is close to zero.

When world money was constrained by gold, it couldn't accumulate infinitely. There is a finite amount of gold to be had and much of it is already above-ground. But the gold standard was abandoned in 1971 and the money supply of the world was liberated from its gold base. Thereafter, we get this tremendous growth in the money supply. It becomes whatever the central banks of the world decide it is going to be, with the US Federal Reserve in the lead because the US dollar is the global reserve currency and most international transactions occur in dollar-denominated contracts. When we get into economic difficulties, the Federal Reserve simply prints more money, which adds to the compounding of the quantity of money in circulation. But then the question is what is that money going to do, and how is it going to be profitably invested? We've seen all sorts of adjustments in the global economy to deal with that problem. There is, for example, what Marx called a realization problem: how on earth can all of this money be reinvested in such a way that it finds a market to generate more profit? Where is that profit going to come from? And how will this address social and environmental problems? While the failure of the dominant political-economic model is clearly visible and political protests are proliferating, there is at this time little consideration given to how the underlying problems might be addressed within or outside of the existing frameworks of economic management of the global capitalist economy. The monstrous imbalances emerging in the global economy cry out for major readjustments. But the other side of the coin is this: capital is too big, too monstrous, too huge to survive. It cannot survive in its current form on its current growth trajectory. On the one hand, we can't do without it, on the other hand, it is on a suicidal path. This is the central dilemma.

There are many contradictions in the capitalist system, and some are more salient than others. The incredible class and social inequalities and collapsing environmental conditions are obvious priorities. But then comes the "too big to fail, too monstrous to survive" contradiction. Neither the social inequality nor environmental degradation issues can be addressed without taking on this underlying contradiction. A socialist and anti-capitalist program will have to negotiate a knife-edge path between preserving that which services the world's population and which appears too big and foundational to fail while confronting the fact that it is becoming too monstrous to survive without sparking geopolitical conflicts that will likely turn the innumerable small wars and internal struggles already raging across the planet into a global conflagration.

This is the core of the problem. In Marx's time, if there was a sudden collapse of capitalism, most people in the world would still have been able to feed themselves and reproduce. They were reasonably self-sufficient in their local area procuring the kinds of things they needed to live and reproduce. People could put some sort of breakfast on their table irrespective of what was going on in the global economy and in global markets. Right now, that's no longer the case in many parts of the world. Most people in the United States, in much of Europe, in Japan, and now increasingly in China, India, Indonesia, and in Latin America are depending more and more on the delivery of food through the circulation of capital. In Marx's time, perhaps 10 percent of the global population was vulnerable to disruptions in the circulation of capital, as opposed to many more who were subject to famines, droughts, epidemics, and other environmental disruptions. The crisis of European capitalism in 1848 was part a product of harvest failures and part produced by a speculative crash focused on railroad finance. Since then, capital operating in the world market has largely eliminated the prospect of starvation due to supposedly natural causes. If there is famine the underlying causes (as opposed to the immediate triggers) can invariably be traced to failures in the social and political system of capitalist governance and distribution. Much of the world's population is now dependent upon the circulation of capital to procure and ensure its food supply, access the fuels and the energy required to support daily life, and to maintain the elaborate structures and equipment of communication that facilitate the coordination of basic production requirements.

Capital, right now, may be too deeply implicated in the reproduction of daily life to fail. The economic consequences and social impacts and costs of a massive and prolonged failure in the continuity of capital circulation will be catastrophic and potentially lethal for a significant portion of the world's population. To be sure, indigenous and peasant populations in the Andean highlands may survive quite well, but if the flow of capital shuts down for any prolonged period, then maybe two-thirds of the world's population would within a few weeks be threatened with starvation, deprived of fuel and light, while being rendered immobile and deprived of almost all capacity to reproduce their conditions of existence effectively. We cannot now afford any kind of sustained and prolonged attack upon or disruption of capital circulation even if the more egregious forms of accumulation are strictly curbed. The kind of fantasy that revolutionaries might once have had – which was that capitalism could be destroyed and burned down overnight and that something different could immediately be built upon the ashes – is impossible today even supposing there ever was a time when such a revolutionary overthrow might have happened. Some form of the circulation of commodities and therefore of money capital has to be kept in motion for some considerable time lest most of us starve. It is in this sense that we might say that capital appears to be now too big to fail. We may aspire to make our own history, Marx observed, but this can never be done under conditions of our own choosing. These conditions dictate a politics that is about sustaining many existing commodity chains and flows while socializing and perhaps gradually modifying them to accommodate to human needs. As Marx noted in his commentary on the Paris Commune,

> in order to work out their own emancipation, and along with it the higher form to which present society is irresistibly tending by its own economical agencies, they [the working classes] will have to pass through long struggles, through a series of historic processes, transforming circumstances and men. They have no ideals to realize, but to set free the elements of the new society with which old collapsing bourgeois society is pregnant.

The task is to identify that which lays latent in our existing society to find a peaceful transition to a more socialist alternative. Revolution is a long process not an event.

2

A Brief History of Neoliberalism

Back in 2005, I wrote a book called *A Brief History of Neoliberalism*. I do not like to advertise my own publications, but it is rather important to recount what has happened since I published that book. The main theme of the book was the way in which political and economic power had been mobilized in the 1970s to try to capture as much accumulation as possible, and as much wealth and power as possible, within the corporate class.

In the 1970s, that class had felt threatened because there was a lot of legislation going through which was anti-corporate: environmental regulations, consumer protections, occupational safety and health, issues of this kind. There was a famous memo sent around by Lewis Powell, who later went on to serve on the Supreme Court. The gist of what he had to say was that "things have gone too far. The anti-capitalist rhetoric has become too strong. We have to counter-attack and we have to mobilize." And all sorts of organizations got together, like the Business Roundtable, the Chamber of Commerce and an assortment of right-wing think tanks that were available or newly set up at that time to reverse the tide of anti-capitalist rhetoric, which was, indeed, becoming very strong.

How this happened was a major theme of the book. Neoliberalism, for me, was always defined as a class project, a project to accumulate more wealth and power within a small elite class. Here we are, many years later, and in fact, that process of accumulating wealth and power in a very small class has gone even further than ever before.

I'm often asked, "Did neoliberalism end in 2007–08? Was that the crisis of neoliberalism, and if so, where are we now?" And that's one of the questions that we ought to seriously consider politically. But to do that, we have to understand a little bit about how neoliberalism, as a project, worked. I recognized, for example, that while it was a project of a small elite of capitalist class and large corporations, it needed a sound popular base. From the 1970s onwards, there was an attempt to capture the Republican Party. There was an attempt to capture a popular base for this project of a small elite. That popular base was largely the religious right, which became increasingly politicized from the 1970s on.

There was also an attempt to come up with a theoretical justification. I do not think, for example, that the capitalists who got together in the 1970s thought about this particularly, but they found at hand an economic doctrine that would be called monetarism or supply-side economics, which was a neat way of saying, "Well, we need to change the dynamic. We need to get the state out of interventions in the economy. We need to create freer markets. We need to get rid of the power of the trades unions, in particular." So, supply-side economics entered into the picture as a convenient economic theory to found the neoliberal project.

This effect was to say that the economy should be managed by controlling the supply conditions, and the supply condition that was most crucial to manage was, of course, that of labor power. Labor was too strong in the 1970s. Labor had strong unions, and in Europe and Britain there were labor parties, and social democratic parties, and even the Democratic Party in the United States was very beholden to big labor. The early phases of neoliberalism were about curbing the power of the unions and "big labor," and trying to reconfigure the political situation to weaken the role of labor by whatever means possible.

In order to do that, there needed to be some way for the corporate elite to attain political power. That meant spending money on elections. There were a lot of controversies in the 1970s about too much money coming into elections – was it justified? There were several Supreme Court cases during those years. And put briefly, it went from a situation where money in elections was regarded as being necessary, but it should be modest, to opening up elections to total monetization. The expenditure of money was ultimately determined and protected by the Supreme Court to be a form of free speech. Therefore, nobody should get in the way of the free flow of money into politics. This allowed the big corporations and the wealthy individuals to increasingly dominate politics.

They also needed to dominate the media, and they started to do that very effectively through the consolidation and centralization of corporate controls and ownership. They needed at some point or other to capture the universities. But in the early 1970s, the student movement was too anti-corporate and too anti-war and the faculty too liberal-leaning for this to be feasible. There was an attempt to surround the universities by think tanks – the Manhattan Institute, the National Bureau of Economic Research, the Olin Foundation, the Heritage Foundation, and the like. All of these institutes were funded by big capital. They produced a stream of publications and a stream of arguments which were against labor, pro-corporate and in favor of freedom of the market and opening up the market to much greater levels of competition. This was the situation that prevailed from the 1970s onwards, and it was a pretty successful project.

By the time you get to the 1990s, labor has been largely disempowered. Most of the regulatory apparatus to control corporations has been dismantled. The Democratic Party under Clinton has become an agent of neoliberal politics. Clinton came into power promising a progressive reform of healthcare and better living conditions for people. But what he ended up giving to the country was the North American Free Trade Agreement (NAFTA) which was an anti-labor agreement. There was nobody from big labor in the room when the agreement was signed. The Democratic Party pulled away from its traditional base in big labor and began to cultivate the cosmopolitan urban professional elites as its new power base.

Clinton gave us NAFTA and the reform of welfare as we knew it. He gave us the incarceration project, which criminalized a lot of black youth. He repealed financial regulations – a crucial piece of legislation that had been in place since the 1930s, called the Glass Steagall Act, was repealed. Clinton was a main agent of the neoliberal project. On the other side of the Atlantic Tony Blair played a similar neoliberal role. We had to collaborate with business rather than be antagonistic, he said.

By the 1990s, the neoliberal project had worked pretty well. If you look at the data on social inequality, what you see is an enormous increase in social inequality across nearly all the major Organisation for Economic Co-operation and Development (OECD) countries – Britain, United States, many European countries. That rising social inequality is documented in Thomas Piketty's book *Capital in the Twenty-First Century*. It is not really a book about capital but about the creation of greater and greater levels of social inequality under capitalism, from the 1970s onwards.

This was what you might call a successful political project. Labor was disempowered. Environmental regulation was not enforced. The regulation on finance was cut back. Then one thinks of the Allende socialist election in Chile and the Pinochet neoliberal counterrevolution in Chile in 1973. We had a whole era, which was led, initially, by Margaret Thatcher and Ronald Reagan in their respective countries, and then other figures around the world.

In the neoliberalism book, I tried to go over all of this, and talk about the state that we were in just after the year 2000. It was a state in which that successful neoliberal project had worked itself out. It seemed that there was very little opposition that was possible. Margaret Thatcher had this famous phrase: "There is no alternative" (TINA). She had taken the view that not only was she about to transform the economy, she wanted to transform peoples' way of thinking and the whole economic culture. The way of thinking that was being promoted was one of individualism, personal responsibility, and self-improvement. We were all supposed to be entrepreneurs of ourselves and to invest in ourselves.

So, if we ended up in poverty, it was because we had not invested correctly in ourselves. If we got into poverty, it was our fault. It was not the system's fault; it was our fault. If we lost our houses to foreclosure, it was not the system's fault, it was our fault. There was this notion of self-reliance. By the time you get to the 1990s, that idea had become dominant. It has, however, a very deep root. This is one of the things that I emphasized quite a lot in the book. The 1960s had seen a very strong movement of people wanting individual liberty, and freedom, and also social justice. That movement of the '68 generation, if you want to call it that, was antagonistic to what capital was about. The response of capital was to say "We give you the individual liberty, and we value the individual liberty too, and we will structure things around individual liberty, particularly in the market, so that you get lots of freedom of choice in the market. But the bargain is that you forget about the social justice."

That was the devil's bargain that the '68 generation was offered by Reagan and Thatcher in the 1970s and 1980s, up to the Clinton era of the 1990s. By the time you get to the 1990s, many people started to accept that if they were running into problems, it was their own fault. That the system was, in fact, going very well. It was going very well for the ultra-rich and the successful entrepreneurs. The ultra-rich were getting richer, and richer, and richer. The gap between what the CEOs were earning and what individual employees were earning was becoming wider, and wider, and wider.

Then came, of course, 2007–08, and that big crisis. It seemed as if the system had failed. Here, I think, we come across a very crucial point to understand what is going on around us right now. In the 1990s, right the way through to the mid-2000s, the public was persuaded that this system was at least viable. When you get to 2007–08, the recognition is that this system is not viable. And furthermore, everybody started to see that the ultra-rich were the ones who had been benefiting. In 2007–08, when the government bailed out the bankers, bailed out Wall Street, gave them everything, and the Wall Street bankers collectively took bonuses of over $30 billion in 2008, for crashing the world's financial system, and everybody at that point said this system is being gamed by the ultra-rich. We start then to see an attack upon what the neoliberal system had been about all along.

But then the big question is: was there really an attack upon the power of capital or was the attack finessed in some way, so that neoliberalism continued? My argument is that neoliberalism did not end in 2007–08. What was lost was its legitimacy and its political legitimacy in particular. The discontent with the system was there.

The discontent became, and has become, deeper, and deeper, and deeper. In other words, people began to be alienated from the whole economic system in which they had their being. But at the same time, the system itself was not changing.

In fact, since 2007–08, the rich have benefited more than anyone else. They've used the doctrine of "never let a good crisis go to waste," and they've actually used it to their own benefit. If you look at the data from Britain and the United States, you will find that the top 1 percent has increased its wealth and power by 14, 15, maybe 20 percent, while everybody else has either remained stagnant or lost since 2008. The neoliberal project has not come to an end. In fact, it has continued. But it has continued under a situation where it is no longer legitimate in the way that it was before. A new form of legitimacy had to be found for the neoliberal project. This new form of legitimacy is something which I think we have to pay very careful attention to.

In 2007–08 there was this crash. The crash was in housing markets. Around 7 million households lost their homes in the United States. When something like that happens, you would expect there to be mass movement on the part of those who have been deprived of their homes. You would expect them to be out on the streets protesting. There was a little bit of that, but by and large, what happened in 2007–08 was that people who lost their homes blamed themselves. The neoliberal culture that had been built up from the 1980s onwards, which was about self-improvement and investment in your own capital, and so on, led people to blame themselves and to internalize the problems. There were plenty of people, of course, in the media and elsewhere, who were all too ready to pile on and blame the victims.

Now, when victims get blamed, there's always a residual, a hidden voice asking, "am I really to blame?" And there's a discomfort, and a feeling of inadequacy. And so, the whole population that was affected by 2007–08 was left in limbo. They saw government attending to the bankers and healing the wounds of the banking industry. But they didn't see anybody coming to help them. They received instead a politics of increasing austerity of public provision and faced hostility as noxious failures. And austerity for what? To pay off the bankers? Or to pay off the ultra-rich? This left the victims with a suspicion that something was wrong.

That suspicion led people to ask the question, "What went wrong in the financial system that we got such a huge crash? And why did it go global?" The typical answer was that "The financial system is so complicated. You can't understand all of these instruments, these things like credit default swaps, and collateralized debt obligations," it is far too complicated for you mere mortals to understand. Everybody started saying, "The financial system is so complicated. Nobody can understand it except the experts."

Then people said, "Well, if only the experts can understand it, how come the experts were so wrong? Why didn't the experts see what might go and ultimately did go wrong?" There was a wonderful moment when the Queen of England, of all people, sat down with a bunch of economists at one of these tea parties at Buckingham Palace and apparently, she turned to the economists and said, "How come you didn't see the crash coming?" The economists just did not know what to say. They called together a meeting of the economic society, and tried to come up with some answers, so that they could go and have tea with Her Majesty next time and say, "Well we understood what went wrong." The only answer they came up with was "We didn't understand systemic risk."

Now, this is an astonishing admission. If there is a system, and there's risk in the system, moreover systemic risk not accidental risk, you would have thought that a lot of people would be paying attention to it. But it turned out that none of the economists, none of the theorists, none of the experts were paying any attention to the mounting risks within the system. The risks, when they finally caused the crisis, caught everybody by surprise. Now this was a default of intellectual capacity and it was a default of imagination. And this meant that there was something really wrong within the system itself, which needed to be corrected. Here is where I think we then stood after 2007–08 in terms of how to start to think about what went wrong, and how to think about legitimizing, actually, what was going on, in terms of the continued advantaging of the ultra-rich through the policies of the government. So what kinds of answers might emerge from all of this?

3

Contradictions of Neoliberalism

I analyzed the neoliberal project through the lens of Marx's *Capital*. I sought to identify the central contradiction of the neoliberal project. There are several dimensions to contradictions in Marx's work, but there is a simple way to look at it. In Volume I of *Capital*, Marx analyzes what happens in a society with strong technological change, and a strong search for profit. He analyzes the "surplus value production" that rests on the exploitation of labor power in production. Therefore, the suppression of the power of labor, which began in the 1970s, corresponded to the analysis that Marx laid out in Volume I of *Capital*.

At the end of Volume I of *Capital*, Marx describes a situation where capitalists, given that they have so much power, can increase the exploitation of the workers and thereby maximize their rate of profit. The maximization of the rate of profit rests on the diminution of the wage. One of the key graphs you'll see in *A Brief History of Neoliberalism* shows that the share of wages in national income has progressively declined since the 1970s. Increases in productivity have not been paralleled by any increase in real wages. Volume I of *Capital* predicts an increasing impoverishment of large segments of the population, increasing unemployment, the creation of disposable populations, and the production of greater precarity within the labor force. This is an analysis that comes out of Volume I of *Capital*.

But if you read Volume II of *Capital*, you get another story because there Marx looks at how capital circulates, and how it relates demand and supply, and how it keeps itself in equilibrium as the system reproduces itself. In order to keep an equilibrium, the wage rate must be stabilized. Put in very simple terms, if you continuously diminish the power of labor, and the wages are going down, then the big question is "Where's the market? What happens to the market?" So that Marx starts to say the Volume I story produces a situation where capitalists are going to face difficulties in the market because they are paying the workers less, and less, and less, and there's less, and less, and less of a market. This is one of the central contradictions of the neoliberal period and the neoliberal era, which is "Where is your market going to come from?"

There are a number of answers to this. One answer lies with geographical expansion. The incorporation of China, Russia, and the ex-Soviet empire countries of Eastern Europe into the global capitalist system opened up huge new markets and possibilities. There are many other ways to fashion an answer for this problem. But the biggest answer of all was give people credit cards. Let them go into debt. Push them into debt. Create ever higher levels of debt.

In other words, if workers don't have enough money to buy a house, then you lend them money to buy a house. And then, the housing market goes up because you've lent the workers money. In the 1990s, more and more money was lent to people who had lower and lower income streams. This was one of the roots of the 2007–08 crisis. Eventually credit was extended to almost everyone no matter their income and ability to service their mortgage. This was no problem while housing prices were rising. If mortgagees got into difficulty they (or their bank) could always sell out at a profit.

But the main question was how could the demand side be managed in a situation where wages were being diminished? As I've suggested, one of the ways to bridge the difference was to expand the credit system. The figures here are actually pretty astounding. In 1970, the total indebtedness in a capitalist society – typical capitalist society – was relatively modest. And most of the indebtedness was not cumulative. It was the sort of thing where you borrow here and you pay back there. So, the net indebtedness was not growing very fast in the 1970s.

But from the 1970s onwards, net debt started to increase in relation to gross domestic product (GDP). And we've now got a situation where the total indebtedness in the world is about 225 percent of the total output of goods and services in the world. Of course, these are just numbers, and it's hard to put them in context, but the context would be that, back in 1980, Mexico got into a debt problem, and it was only indebted up to about 80 percent or 90 percent of its GDP. So back then, to be 80 percent or 90 percent in debt was actually seen as a crisis situation that had to be addressed. But now the world is three or four times more in debt than was the case back then and nobody seems to be too bothered by it. Thus, one of the things we've seen over this period has been a growing indebtedness.

The other thing that I thought was terribly important to understand during the 1980s was that the neoliberal project could not survive without having a strong state. Now this, ideologically, is rather complicated because a lot of the rhetoric about neoliberalism is "Get the state out. Get rid of the state. The state is a problem so we've got to get rid of state intervention." "Government," Ronald Reagan famously said, "is not the solution ... Government is the problem."

But the state did not get out. Its function changed from supporting people by creating welfare structures, such as healthcare, education, and a wide range of social services, to supporting capital. The state became an active agent in support of and sometimes even subsidizing capital. From the 1980s onwards we see all sorts of games played by the state in support of capital.

A recent example was when Amazon decided to set up a second servicing center it invited cities and local governments to submit bids. "What will you give us?" said Amazon. Here's one of the richest companies in the world, which says, basically, it needs to be subsidized to operate. New Jersey was going to offer this, and somebody else was going to offer that. It is now normal for corporations to be subsidized out of the public purse to do their work. New York City and State offered all kinds of inducements but the local population in this case revolted and so Amazon was forced to withdraw. But this is unusual.

Foxconn, which has just agreed to set up a factory in Wisconsin, has been given $4 billion worth of incentives from the state government. The state government, instead of putting $4 billion into education, and healthcare, and other things that people need, gives $4 billion to Foxconn. The state then argues, "Well, this creates jobs," but, actually, it's not going to create that many jobs, and when you figure it out, it turns out there's just probably about $20,000 per job, which is being offered in subsidy. The state has moved away from supporting people to supporting corporate enterprise by any means that it can, by taxation arrangements, by direct subsidies, the provision of infrastructures, and the evasion of regulatory constraints.

For this to happen requires a strong state. You cannot have a weak state. One of the things that I mentioned in the neoliberalism book was the emerging alliance between neoliberalism and neoconservatism. The "neo-cons," as they were called in the 1990s, formed a strong faction in government. They came to power in the Bush Junior administration, which was very much focused on combining the neoconservative ethic, as represented by Donald Rumsfeld and Dick Cheney, with neoliberal economic principles. The neo-cons stood for a strong state, which was a militarized state. And this state was also going to support the neoliberal project of capital.

It so happened that the militarized state also went to war with Iraq, which turned out disastrously. But the point here was that the neoliberal project meshed with a strong neoconservative state. This alliance was very significant and strengthened over time as neoliberalism lost its popular legitimacy.

This state support for big capital did not go away in 2007–08. During the Bush years, for a variety of reasons, the neoconservative project increasingly lost legitimacy because of the Iraq war. The neo-cons got us into the Iraq war. They got us into foreign adventurism. By the end of the Bush administration, the alliance between neo-cons and neoliberalism was frayed. The neo-cons were really finished. The main participants, like Condoleezza Rice and Rumsfeld, just faded into the background of politics. This meant that the legitimacy which the neo-con movement provided to the neoliberal politics of the Bush era disappeared. Then came the crisis of 2007–08. The state had to stand strong and rescue big capital. This was the big story of 2007–08.

We got out of the crisis internally within the United States by strong state power being mobilized out of the ashes of the neoconservative project. This may have been ideologically inconsistent with the neoliberal argument against strong state intervention. But the state had no option but to intervene on behalf of capital, but not on behalf of the people. Given a choice between supporting the banks and the financial institutions, on the one hand, or supporting the people, on the other, the clear choice was to support financial institutions. This emerged as one of the key rules of the neoliberal political game, which was ruthlessly followed in the years to come.

The crisis of 2007–08 could have been resolved by offering massive subsidies to the homeowners who were threatened with foreclosure. There would then have been no massive foreclosure movement. You would have saved the financial system that way, rather than saving the financial system and having people lose their houses. So why was this obvious solution never tried?

Having people lose their houses was actually quite a good thing from the standpoint of capital. Because then there were a lot of foreclosed houses out there that all the hedge funds and private equity groups could buy up for almost nothing and then make a killing later on to a degree that the housing market revived. Actually, one of the biggest landlords in the United States right now is Blackstone, which is a private equity company. It bought up all of the foreclosed housing that it could and turned them into a very profitable venture. It made a killing out of the catastrophe in the housing market. Steven Schwartzman, head of Blackstone, became one of the richest persons in the world almost overnight.

This all became clear in 2007–08. The state was not meeting the needs of people. It was responding to the needs of big capital. There was no longer a neo-con movement around that had credibility.

So where was political legitimacy going to come from? How was legitimacy going to be constructed in the wake of 2007–08? This leads us to one of the keys to what has been happening in more recent times. I have already suggested that people were left behind in 2007–08. People felt that nobody was willing to help them or cared about their situation. We were at the tail-end of nearly three decades of de-industrialization that had destroyed many communities and left many people bereft of decent employment opportunities. People were alienated, and alienated populations tend to be very unstable. They tend to be morose in parts and depressed in others. Some of the consequences are drug addiction and alcoholism. The opioid epidemic took hold and the rate of personal suicides picked up. Life expectancy has actually fallen in many parts of the country, so that the state of the population is not good at all. The population as a whole feels hard done by.

At this point, the question starts to be asked: "who's to blame for all of this?" The last thing that the big capitalists and their media want is for people to start to blame capitalism and the capitalists. This had happened before, back in 1968 and '69. People had started to blame capital and the corporations. The result was an anti-capital movement.

In 2011, of course, there was the Occupy movement, which came along and pointed the finger at Wall Street and blamed them. People started to think, "Well, you know, maybe there's something going on here, which is that the bankers are being privileged and they've, in effect, done a lot of criminal activity and none of them have gone to jail." The only country in the world that sends big bankers (as opposed to a few rogue underlings) to jail is Iceland.

Wall Street was actually made rather nervous when Occupy pointed at the one percent, saying that's where the problem lies. Immediately, all the big institutions, which, by then, were well dominated by capital, constructed a range of alternative explanations, such as "the problem is immigrants" or "the lazy welfare population" (often racially coded) or "unfair China competition," or "the problem is people who have been not looking after and investing in themselves properly." The opioid epidemic was constructed as a tragic failure of individual will.

You start to hear these rumors and rumblings within the mainstream press, and within many of the institutions that are controlled by the far right and the alternative right, which, at that point, suddenly becomes sponsored through the Tea Party, and through the

Koch brothers, and some factions of big capital sponsored by a huge flow of money into purchasing electoral power, dominating state governments, as well as the federal government.

This was a continuation of a 1970s trend, which entailed the consolidation of capitalist class power around a political project. But this time it is the immigrants to blame, or foreign competition and the state of the world market, too much stifling regulation, and the like for all the problems. Blame anything but capital!

Ultimately, we end up with Donald Trump, who is paranoid, erratic and a bit of a psychopath. But look at what he has done. He has deregulated as much as he possibly can. He has destroyed the Environmental Protection Agency, which is one of the things the big capitalists have been after since the 1970s. He had a tax reform which gave almost everything to the top 1 percent and to the big corporations and the bond-holders, and almost nothing to the people. The deregulation of mineral exploitation, the opening up of federal lands, and all the rest of it, is assured. This is a set of pure neoliberal policies. Only tariff wars and maybe anti-immigration policies are outside of the neoliberal playbook. From the standpoint of the economy, Trump is basically following the neoliberal gospel.

But how is the economic policy justified? How is it legitimized? He seeks to legitimize it by a nationalist, anti-immigrant rhetoric. This is a classic mode in which capital can proceed. We see the Koch brothers dominating electoral politics with their money power, dominating the media through Breitbart, Fox News, and all the rest of it. And they are pursuing this neoliberal project (without the tariff wars and anti-immigration) unashamedly.

At this point, however, the capitalist class is not as consolidated and unified as it was back in the 1970s. There are wings of the capitalist class that see that there is something clearly wrong with the neoliberal economic model. And there are aspects of what Trump is about, for instance, tariffs, anti-free trade and anti-immigration, which are not necessarily what the Koch brothers want. This is not what the capitalist class as a whole wants. We have a situation where the capitalist class itself is a little frayed right now, but you can see that the response to 2007–08 was directly linked to the rise of this "blame somebody else other than capital" movement, which was a desperate move on the part of the capitalist class during these years. So far it has been successful. But it is also clearly fragile and unstable. And unstable populations, particularly alienated populations, can head in any number of different political directions.

4

The Financialization of Power

Let me go back to an aspect of this whole history which is I think significant and deserves to be looked at in its own right, which is the increasing financialization of everything and the incredible increase in financial power. There are some interesting features of this, because historically finance was often viewed as a parasitic function, as something that was not productive of anything. Up until the 1970s, financial activities were not included in national accounts. They were not part of the measure of GDP, because they were seen simply as transactional rather than productive activities. But with the growth of financial power what we see is an increasing attempt on the part of the financiers to say that they are productive, and that therefore what they do should be included in national accounts. This has become a very big issue, as you can imagine, with Brexit in Britain, because the City of London is supposed to be productive for the British economy. Everybody wants to hang onto the role of the City of London. Back in 1970 it would not have been classified as productive. It would have been classified as transactional and circulating activity, and not, therefore, directly productive of anything. Britain produced cars and things and the financial stuff was irrelevant. But Lloyd Blankfein, the past head of Goldman Sachs, vociferously maintained that not only does Goldman do "God's work," but that it is, in fact, one of the most productive sectors of the US economy. The workers of Goldman Sachs are, he says, some of the most productive workers in the world.

This poses the interesting question of the value of financial services. Could we all just live on financial services? You cannot eat them, wear them, or live in them. So, the case for financial services being largely parasitic is actually quite strong. If they are classified as parasitic and unproductive – which was a common theme in the rhetoric of Occupy Wall Street – then they will lose their privileged position both politically and economically. But right now, Goldman Sachs maintains it is so productive that for New York to try and exist without Goldman Sachs would be to court an economic disaster. Restrictive regulation of its activities has had negative consequences for employment and growth. The further deregulation of financial services has been a long-standing focus of agitation in New York. Right before the crash of 2007–08 there was strong pressure by the then mayor of New York, Michael Bloomberg, to further deregulate financial services in New York to make them more competitive with London. Further deregulation would unleash the latent productive capacity that was already in place. Productive capacity, it was said, was being held back and held down by all this regulatory apparatus. Well, the crash came, and then the regulations came, in the form of the Dodd-Frank financial reform law. And what do we now see? There is this not so subtle campaign to chip away at the Dodd-Frank law and further deregulate financial services. The Trump administration, which has continued in the tradition of hiring ex-Goldman Sachs' executives to run the US Treasury Department, has been very happy to go along.

Is finance productive of value? If so, in what ways is it productive of value? There is here, I think, one very interesting feature, which I have to go back to Marx to understand. Capital is always about growth, and it's always about compound growth – 3 percent compound growth is, it seems, the happy norm. But compound growth produces an exponential growth curve, which goes faster and faster and faster. The famous story is the person who invented the game of chess and was offered a reward by the king. The person who invented it said, "I want one grain of rice on the first square, and then I want it doubled on every square." The king agreed and thought that no problem. But by the time you got to about the 34th square, there was no rice left in the world. That is what compound interest does. You go from 1 to 2 to 4 to 8 to 16 to 32 to 64, and so on. You just go down that track. Capital has been growing at a compound rate of around 3 percent a year since 1750 or so. On average a little less than that historically, because periods of depression such as that of the 1930s interrupted the growth path. But let's say it is 3 percent compound rate of growth. When Marx was writing, 3 percent compound rate of growth on everything that was going on in just Western Europe and Britain and maybe the Eastern Seaboard of the United States. This was no big deal. However, 3 percent compound rate of growth right now, going forward, is a huge, huge deal. There is a real problem of how to absorb this compound rate of growth. You have got to find and continuously expand investment opportunities for more and more money.

Right now, the global GDP is close to $80 trillion. So, we now need to find new investment opportunities for an extra $80 trillion hopefully yielding at least a 3 percent profit over the next 25 years. Back in 2000, we only needed to absorb $40 trillion. In another 20 years, we're going to be talking about $160 trillion. The global economy needs to double in size every two decades or so. What form can such an extraordinary expansion take? Can the economy expand physically? Look at its expansion physically over the last 40 to 50 years. The whole of the ex-Soviet Union empire has come into the capitalist system, China has joined the capitalist system. Many countries that were rather quiescent in the past, and didn't have too much capitalist development, like Indonesia and India, are now fully integrated into the expanding global capitalist economy. A compound rate of physical growth is potentially catastrophic for environmental and other reasons.

My favorite piece of information on this is the consumption of cement in China. In two years after 2012, the Chinese consumed twice as much cement as the United States had consumed in the previous 100 years. If that is what compound growth means physically, then this means a disaster down the road. In 60 years' time we will be up to our necks in cement. So there's a real, real problem about how the system is going to expand. Can it expand in terms of commodities produced and consumed? Can it expand in terms of productive activity and surplus value production? Can it expand in terms of money power? The only one of these options that is in principle limitless is money. It merely entails just adding zeros to the world's money supply.

This is in effect what quantitative easing by the world's central banks does. The world's money supply has expanded exponentially since the 1970s. Such an expansion can in principle go on indefinitely. But if you have more and more money in the world, the question then arises as to what can it be used for and what can it buy? It is hard for all that new money to go into real investment. When the banks were bailed out with a lot more money after 2007–08, the hope was that much of it would go to increase productive activity. But less than 20 percent of it went into that. The rest was used to buy back stocks, invest in asset values in the stock market or buy up natural resource assets (including land and property). So, it didn't go to anything productive. It mainly went into monetary instruments and speculating on land values and property values. Here is an interesting thing. One of the responses to the crash of 2007–08 – which began in property markets – was to revitalize and accelerate speculation in key property markets. In China, there has been a lot of crazy activity in the property markets. About 15 percent of China's growth has been about building houses since the crisis of 2008 in China's export industries. Somebody in the Federal Reserve Bank of San Francisco once said, "The United States has a long history of getting out of crises by building houses and filling them with things." And if you look at the property markets of all major metropolitan areas around the world, there's been an incredible boom in property values, to the point where large segments of the population have no affordable place to live. Trying to find a place to live in New York City, right now, for a population that is trying to live on $50,000 a year – forget it, there's no place to live. The crisis of affordable housing is real and widespread.

This is the insanity of the situation. The monetary side has picked up very quickly since 2007–08, without very much "progress" on the physical side. Now in some parts of the world there has been progress, but by and large most of the recent monetary expansion has actually ended up disproportionately in the hands of the wealthy.

This has particularly been true with policies of quantitative easing, where central banks (the Federal Reserve in the United States, the Bank of England, the European Central Bank and the Japanese Central Bank) buy up liabilities of mortgages and bonds held by the commercial banks. The central banks pay cash. This increases liquidity (free money) in the economy while in effect storing the mortgages and bonds which would otherwise weigh down the activity of the commercial banks. This is quantitative easing. This was one of the key responses after 2007–08. The world's central banks increased the global money supply. But this extra money did not necessarily flow into productive activity; it largely flowed into the purchase of asset values instead.

Most received opinion held that quantitative easing basically benefited the upper classes at the expense of the lower classes. The Bank of England did a detailed study that showed that the lower classes got proportionately more out of quantitative easing than the upper classes. It was only at the very end of the article that you got to understand what this meant: the lower 10 percent of the population on average over five years received something like £3,000 extra. The upper 10 percent received £325,000 extra. But the rate of improvement of the lower classes was higher than the rate of improvement of the upper classes. This is really a commentary on how poor the bottom 10 percent actually are. What would you rather have: a 10 percent rate of return on $10 or a 5 percent rate of return on a million dollars? That was what, in effect, was happening. The upper classes have increased the mass of their wealth and power immensely, while the bottom 10 percent can afford an extra couple of cups of coffee a week through this quantitative easing. But the headline of the report was "The poor actually benefited more, relatively speaking, than the rich." This distinction between the rate and mass of increase is very, very important. The big corporations may have relatively low rates of return, but you can see that the absolute mass of return for Exxon, or whoever, is a huge amount of money, compared to, say, a relatively high rate of return of a family restaurant struggling to pay rising rents and delivery costs in Manhattan.

Relative shifts in the disposition of the mass are indicators of how the money side of things has become more and more significant. This is where increasing social inequality lies. The monetary side of things even enters into how corporations function. We think of General Motors, for example, as a company that makes automobiles. But one of the most successful parts of the company was General Motors Acceptance Corporation, which actually is about lending money for auto purchases. It became so big and successful that it ultimately turned into an independent bank. Many of the big auto corporations make more money out of financial operations than they do out of making cars. I saw some data on airlines recently, and it turns out that the airlines, by hedging on fuel prices and messing around like that, make more money out of their financial manipulations than they do by actually flying people anywhere. Many production corporations engage in financial manipulations. To do so depends on the prospects for a good rate of return. But that means you need a corporation to move fast, to be very sophisticated, and to have access to good information so as to leverage funds from one thing to another to maximize income and the rate of return between this and that. The leadership of many corporations are increasingly drawn from financial rather than engineering experts. Governments and local states often help to structure helpful financial bargains. For example, a bank can borrow from the Federal Reserve at, say, a rate of 1.5 percent, and turn around and put the money in treasuries at 3 percent. In so doing, the banks are not making anything other than money. But this became very common after 2007–08. All this money was pumped into the system, but very little of it went into productive activity. It mainly went into game-playing in the financial system. This included asset purchases. There has been a lot of what is called "land grabbing" going on around the world. I saw a report that the Harvard University endowment is becoming heavily involved in land purchases or leases in Latin America. Others are heavily involved in Africa, where land prices are shooting up.

So, we're moving into this speculative economy, which is hard to legitimize as productive activity. But there is also considerable difficulty right now in understanding the intricate complexities of the financial system. Behind it all, we see the emergence of a distinctive investor class (e.g. hedge and private equity funds), whose only interest is getting a high rate of return by whatever means possible without any political, social, or economic restraints.

Chief amongst these investors are the pension funds. The pension funds are sitting there saying, "I want a high rate of return," and they go out and ask, "Where can we get the high rate of return? A land grab in Africa?" My pension fund, TIAA, is reportedly involved in land grabs in Latin America. I don't like it, and I protest. But then management says the fiduciary obligation of a pension fund is to get the highest rate of return possible, and if the highest rate of return exists by land grabs in Latin America that's what we have to do. Otherwise, they say, we can be accused of not meeting our fiduciary obligation. We have constructed an insane economy right now, which is so entirely financialized as to forget about production, at the same time as it is increasingly loaded down with debts that either foreclose upon the future or turn out to be unpayable.

In Marx's view, there is always a parasitic element within the financial sector, but there's also a constructive element. We need the financial system in order to smooth out all of the different turnover times in buying and selling of commodities. There are many financial functions that are very useful and helpful in coordinating capital flows. For example, there used to be mutual aid societies, which were small savings and loan institutions, where local people could put their money and they would get a small rate of interest, but then that money could be lent out to somebody in the community to buy a house. Most people would accept that this is a benevolent use of the credit system. The credit system enabled people to raise some money collectively to undertake much needed projects (like building a hospital). There is a constructive side of the credit system. But then there is this insane speculative side like buying up land in Brazil for purposes of speculation. The state should enter in and control the speculative side while facilitating the benevolent side. But the speculative side is, of course, what the capitalists favor, particularly if it offers a higher rate of return. The capitalists seek to abolish state interventions and regulatory controls. Right now, they are trying to get further deregulation of the financial system, so a big battle is about to be fought, I think, over the question of what's going on with financial services and to what degree they are productive. The next election in the United States will pose that question and you can see already what the big money favors. And Trump is delighted to give it to them.

Goldman Sachs' employees are unproductive workers. We need to proclaim that to the heavens. The best we can say of them is that they are unproductive but necessary. We should not throw out the baby with the bathwater. We need within the framework of capitalism, a decent and well-regulated credit system. It needs to be organized and regulated as a public utility, providing credit for adequate and appropriate social functions and needs. We need it to invest in long-term projects with future benefits such as physical and social infrastructures in, say, education. In other words, we need an adequate credit system and credit institutions to help define and fund the future. That is for sure. We do not, however, need Goldman Sachs. Goldman Sachs has provided the Secretary of the Treasury of the United States since around the 1990s. So, it is in effect Goldman Sachs that has been running the economic policy of the United States in the interest of who? Goldman Sachs. And that's what is at the heart of the neoliberal project. We need to resurrect the rhetoric of Occupy Wall Street, which highlights the parasitic speculative elements within the credit system. It is vital to understand what is and what is not productive in the financial system. This is an intellectual and theoretical challenge as well as a practical question.

Finance and debt are a claim on future labor. Indebted students understand that. They've got $100,000 of debt and they've got to spend 10, 15 years working to pay it off, before they can have a life they can call their own. This is their future labor. It also is our collective future. We are moving into a situation of debt slavery, debt peonage, where so many of us are so much in debt. This connects back to something I mentioned earlier. As wages have been falling in relative terms, so demand had to be maintained by increasing resort to credit. The capitalist system survives by extending and expanding the credit system. The growth of credit is the growth of capital. This is our present dilemma. Plainly, this cannot go on forever yet it must go on in order for capital to survive. What might be done about it will be taken up in a future chapter.

5

The Authoritarian Turn

The fact that the poor stay poor and the rich get rich is something that, in the Leonard Cohen song, everybody knows and, furthermore, "that's how it goes." But if everybody knows this then why does "everybody" not do something about it?

The interesting question for me is, what is it that everybody actually does know about our current conjuncture? Consider, for example, the election results that came out on October 8, 2019 in Brazil. What happened was that a guy called Jair Bolsonaro got 46 percent of the vote in the first round of the elections. This was 10 percent more than the polls were predicting, so he did far better than was expected. Against him, coming in number two, was the Workers' Party candidate who got around 29 percent of the vote, and then a bunch of other candidates, so there had to be a run-off, but it was pretty clear that Bolsonaro very likely would prevail in the second round of the elections.

Now, there are a number of things that are interesting about this result, because Bolsonaro is a slightly off-color, bigoted, and unpredictable right-wing candidate. To begin with, the results sparked a huge rally on the Brazilian stock exchange. Stocks went up by 6 percent the next day. The Brazilian real improved by 3 percent on world markets at a time when emerging markets were generally having a hard time. The commercial response to Bolsonaro's position was very positive. The big question is, why? After all, there was nothing in Bolsonaro's record that suggested that he was particularly pro-business. As a congressman, he had been a wild-card person on his own in the far right. He had run in the election mainly on a platform of ending corruption, which would threaten many businesses as well as politicians.

Ending corruption, or as we call it in Washington, "draining the swamp," is becoming a bit of a political gambit these days. There's a big difference, however, between dealing with corruption and using corruption as a means to go after your opponents. In Brazil, to be sure, there seems to be a lot of corruption around. But there's no question that it is being used essentially to emasculate the left rather than to go after the right. President Dilma was thrown out as president as a result of a minor corruption charge. It was simply that she manipulated the statistical data. It wasn't personal corruption. The person who went after her ended up in jail for corruption, and the new president who took Dilma's place was on the record as saying some very, very corrupt things. But nobody went after him presumably because he was a conservative. He also conspired to have Lula imprisoned for corruption, which was to say the least a dubious case. So, when Bolsonaro says he's going after corruption, pretty clearly, he was going to go after corruption in the Worker's Party and on the left. But this is something which is going on these days worldwide. The Chinese, for example, have a very big program against corruption now and it's not clear whether this is against opponents or whether it's really dealing with the root causes of the corruption that does certainly exist, particularly at the local level of Chinese politics.

Bolsonaro also expresses admiration for the military dictatorship which existed in Brazil in the 1970s and 1980s. The military, he says, assured security (of a certain sort). Bolsonaro argued that this was what might be needed to provide security for the population and to curb the out of control criminal activity particularly in the urban favelas where drug dealing and gangs were supposedly dominant. Bolsonaro suggested that he would bring back the military if necessary, to deal with these problems. He also expressed admiration for the president of the Philippines, Duterte, who had resorted to extra-juridical means to deal with drug gangs and criminality. If you come across a drug dealer, you just shoot him dead and that's it. So, this is the kind of person that Bolsonaro is. To cap it all, he was on record as saying all kinds of misogynistic things, nasty and demeaning things about women and people of color of the sort that we in the United States have gotten used to with President Trump. This earned Bolsonaro the nickname of "Trump of the Tropics." This is the political platform on which Bolsonaro finally got elected.

So the question is, why would all the financiers and the Brazilian stock market rally behind him and say, "This is great. This is what we want and this is what we need?" Well, it turns out that Bolsonaro has a financial advisor, an economist called Paulo Guedes trained in Chicago. Note that well: *Chicago!* Remember, it was Chicago that provided the Chicago Boys to General Pinochet in the wake of the coup in 1973 in Chile in which the socialist president Salvador Allende was ousted and the economy was reimagined in terms of Chicago economic theory. This was when the Chicago Boys became very significant in the first wave of neoliberalization, which was unleashed in Latin America through the Pinochet coup. Here we are some 40 years later in the presence of a Chicago economist who says he is in favor of privatization, of fiscal austerity and budgetary balances at the expense of social programs for the poor and, in particular, at the expense of the one big program that the Workers' Party had set up. This was something called the Bolsa Familia, which was a subsidy to low-income populations provided that they sent their kids to school. This delivered quite a bit of purchasing power to the lower classes in Brazil. Guedes favors pension reforms. The Brazilian state pension system is considered far too generous and it needed to be curbed. He is also in favor of privatization of all the state assets. He is, in short, in favor of a classic neoliberal program. This was what the stock market was celebrating. They did not care about Bolsonaro personally. They cared about Guedes becoming finance minister and the neoliberal policies that he would implement. When he took up his post as Minister of Finance he announced that he would follow in the footsteps of Pinochet's Chile.

What is disturbing about this is that there seems to be an alliance emerging between neoliberal economics, on the one hand, and right-wing populism, on the other. This idea is supported by several comparative examples. Take the right-wing party that has emerged in Germany since 2013 which is anti-immigrant, xenophobic, and nationalist in its posture. It arose from almost nothing in 2013 to now being the third largest party in the Bundestag. It had to stand for some sort of economic program. When they were asked, they simply said it is "ordoliberalism," which is a German version of neoliberalism. This version does not rely entirely on a free market ideology. It is about state-guided free markets. Actually, state-guided free markets have been at the center of the European version of neoliberalism in general as well as the German version of neoliberalism all along. In practice, of course, most countries that embrace neoliberal ideology rely upon a lot of state support. Anyway, the right-wing nationalist Alternative for Deutschland Party declared that its economic policy is the German version of neoliberalism.

Here you have two clear examples of far-right populist political movements embracing what might be called neo-fascist, even Nazi propaganda in the German case, and advocating neoliberalism. It starts to look as if there is an alliance emerging then between these alternative populist right movements and the neoliberal project. Is this what is happening in the United States right now?

Trump is certainly articulating a far-right alternative. He does not reject white supremacist and neo-Nazi influences as we saw in Charlottesville. He doesn't deny the alternative right politics of Steve Bannon. To what degree is he also committed to the perpetuation of neoliberalism? It may be an uneasy connection but it is still a connection.

If I am right and neoliberalism has always been a project of the upper classes and the capitalist class and it is primarily a project to sustain and if possible to augment upper class wealth and power, and if the whole history of neoliberalism has been about that and if it has worked out so that the rich have become inevitably richer and the poor have become either stagnant or have lost, then the success of the neoliberal project is undeniable given the evidence of increasing social inequality wherever neoliberal policies have been pursued This is the history we really need to look at.

It is hard in these times to give clear definitions of class structure particularly when we're looking at the concept of the working class because we have so much temporary employment and so much employment in the service sector. The factories are not there in the same way, at least in the United States. They've all gone to China.

The working class has been broken up and divided in all sorts of ways in the advanced capitalist countries.

But there is no problem defining the capitalist class. We know who they are and what they are about. Take the example of the Koch brothers. Now, the Koch brothers inherited their class position and their industrial empire. Koch Industries is a very large private company. They are one of the biggest corporations in the United States. They are a chemical corporation but also a materials corporation. It is said that almost everything we use these days probably has a piece of Koch brothers' product in it.

So they have very wide and broad industrial interests. They are hugely profitable and the Koch brothers themselves are hugely wealthy. What kinds of politics do the Koch brothers follow? The answer is they are classically neoliberal in some ways. They believe in free markets and free trade. They verge upon the libertarian side of neoliberalism. They want fiscal rectitude on the part of the state. They do not want the state intervening. They do not like state regulation and the like, but they are true to their colors in the sense that they also have some somewhat progressive positions. They believe in proper immigration. They believe in, for example, prison reform, and they believe that tariffs are not a good idea. They have attacked Trump over his conflict with China.

The two first of these, immigration and prison reform, have a lot to do with deregulating and opening up the labor market, which of course is of great interest always to the capitalist class. Having free, open labor markets and the fact that a lot of ex-prisoners could not work their way back into the labor force because of the various restrictions they've faced meant that there was a certain inflexibility in the labor force which the Koch brothers didn't like. So, they have some seemingly progressive positions amidst these other commitments to free market and free trade. In the early stages, the Koch brothers helped to fund the Tea Party. They supported the Republican Party very, very strongly and have supported it to their own advantage. One of the Koch brothers[1] went on record as saying that

---

[1]. One of the brothers, David Koch, died recently in August 2019.

the last five years have been the best five years ever for Koch Industries and for their particular interests.

Now, it's interesting they said five years, because that goes back beyond – before – the Trump election, and of course it refers to the tail end of the Obama presidency when the Republicans controlled all the instruments in Congress and were able to stop almost any kind of regulatory intervention on the part of the administration. They were able to stop any kind of expansion of the budget. During those years, the questions of not extending the debt limit, balancing the budget, and reducing taxes became prominent items in the political equation. There were many things of this sort which prevented government from introducing more regulations (e.g. around the environment). For the Koch brothers, this was absolutely fine. The only thing that Obama could do was to legislate by executive order. This was roundly criticized by the Republican Congress, saying he was going beyond the authority of the presidency by, for example, banning the mining on federal lands and measures of that kind. Obama issued a whole series of regulatory orders about immigration, about mining, environment, and the like, which were not to the Koch brothers' liking. But what can be done by executive order can be undone by executive order, so when Trump came in, one of the first things he did was to reverse almost all of Obama's executive orders. This was great for the Koch brothers. Climate change, for example, could no longer be talked about. The Environmental Protection Agency wasn't allowed even to mention the topic. Regulatory controls on mining on federal lands were reduced. Drilling in the Arctic was opened up. Off-shore drilling was opened up. Basically all the regulatory apparatus of finance was gradually chipped away through executive order, and of course the executive orders of the administration on immigration have also come into play.

As far as the Koch brothers were concerned, the politics of the past five years have been extremely favorable to them, apart from the two domestic issues which they are very much interested in – immigration and prison reform. They also got upset at Trump's tariff policies which are, in any case, not part of the neoliberal playbook. But all in all, the Koch brothers have done well out of Trump's presidency and Republican control of Congress. They have a very large political action committee which has been active for some time. They put $100 million into the Republican campaign to maintain control of both houses of Congress. But they also supported some conservative Democrats to help counter the leftward drift of certain factions within the Democratic Party.

The Koch brothers are fierce supporters of the neoliberal project. They are not supporting those Republican candidates who are strongly against immigration reform and who support the tariff wars the Trump administration is pushing. From the standpoint of their libertarian politics and from the standpoint of business interests in general, neither the tariff wars nor immigration controls are a good idea. They interfere with the free flows of goods and services and also of labor power. The support for the Trump push on tariffs comes as much from Democrats as from Republicans. The tariff question has now been resolved between Mexico and Canada with cross-party support. There's a lot of noise about how successful this has been from the standpoint of the United States, but actually, it's not that successful and it's not that great. There's noise about many new prospective trade agreements. There's already a new tariff agreement with South Korea and one now gradually emerging with the Europeans and we'll probably see that accomplished. The one place where there's not going to be a strong and binding tariff agreement is China, and clearly Trump is going to go after China and that's probably OK to some extent with some levels of business and the Democratic Party. But a lot of businesses in the United States as well as farmers don't like the China tariffs either.

The Trump administration is pulling back on the tariff question probably for electoral reasons. But the one area in which the Trump administration pushed hard was tax reform. The 2017 tax reform was a huge giveaway to the corporations, a huge giveaway in which Koch Industries would have benefited immensely, for example, and not only the Industries, but also the wealthy individuals associated with such industries. This is, again, one of the areas in which the Trump politics and the interests of the capitalist class have overlapped very clearly. Look at the picture. The Koch brothers are interested in tax reform and tax benefits. They've got it. They're interested in deregulation of everything, and they've got it, from environment to regulation of finance. They've pretty much got what they want. This is exactly the sort of politics that is occurring in Brazil. It is also the kind of politics you will find in Poland and Hungary as well as in India under Modi. The far right is unified in its support for neoliberal projects and for the increasing concentration and centralization of wealth in society, even as it supports ratcheting up the repression of opposition movements.

The result is that the Koch brothers et al. become wealthier by the minute. But they then use some of that wealth to launch huge philanthropic ventures. This is the way in which the rich justify their wealth. When you visit the Natural History Museum in New York City and stand in the Hall of the Dinosaurs you are in the Koch brothers' donation hall. When the kids look at the dinosaurs they see it is sponsored by the Koch brothers, which is very good PR for the Koch brothers as being good citizens because they're supporting this kind of thing. Go to the Lincoln Center and watch the ballet in the Koch Auditorium.

The rich play this huge philanthropic game to cultivate public support and public awareness and the development of a certain kind of public culture and certain ways of thinking and knowing.

I have been using the Koch brothers as emblematic of what the capitalist class is about. I don't think it is hard in these times to define the capitalist class and what it is about. You look at the Koch brothers. But you could also look at Michael Bloomberg. Here is where things get interesting. The capitalist class is not homogeneous. They may all support free markets, free trade, freedom from regulation, privatization, fiscal rectitude, and all the rest of it, so they're all homogeneous about that, but then they have their own particular kinds of concerns.

For instance, the Koch brothers hate environmental regulation. They refuse and inhibit discussion about climate change. They are very happy with what Donald Trump says about that and the fact that Donald Trump puts in charge of the Environmental Protection Agency (EPA) somebody who is a right-wing nonentity and who hates environmental protection and who seeks to turn the EPA into a dead institution. Ever since Ronald Reagan, the tactic has been to turn the EPA into a non-functional organization. To abolish it would be too much but to de-fang it is easy. Michael Bloomberg, on the other hand, takes the climate change question seriously. So, Michael Bloomberg put in, it is said, something like $100 million to support Democratic candidates in the 2018 election who favored environmental regulation and policies to mitigate carbon emissions.

When I talk about neoliberalism and the capitalist class, I am not talking about an entirely homogeneous capitalist class. There are differences between them. Bloomberg is in favor of environmental regulation; but not financial regulation. The Koch brothers are not in favor of either form of regulation. Bloomberg is not in favor of a large segment of the federal government being given over to the support of the needs of low-income populations and the Koch brothers agree with him on that too. Bloomberg differs with the Koch brothers and many others over climate change and gun control but not on the fundamentals of support for capitalism.

A relatively small number of super-wealthy people and corporations effectively run American politics. It often looks as if we have only one political party in the United States. We have two wings of that same political party. Let's call it The Party of Wall Street. One half of the party is funded and run by the Koch brothers and their ilk, and that's the Republican part. The other half is funded by Michael Bloomberg, Tom Steyer, George Soros, and others of their ilk, which is the Democratic Party side. Both wings depend on financing from the capitalist class. Both of them broadly support the neoliberal project in general with specific divergences, particularly over climate change and management. Both wings support higher education but each has a different kind of education in mind. The neoliberal education, the entrepreneurial education, the cultivation of entrepreneurial spirit in schools on a meritocratic basis, and the like, is one wing. The cultivation of social responsibility and self-reliance is another wing. Both wings support social and cultural projects, but again of different sorts. Both of them are on board with a limited kind of multiculturalism. They both tend to support limited social concerns about the rights of women (but not too far) and gay rights (again not too far).

There is a configuration of economic power which is intervening in politics, but which finds itself right now in a situation of what to do about far-right ethno-nationalist politics and even neo-Nazi politics. The trend towards neo-military dictatorship politics in the case of Brazil is garnering some support in the business community though not necessarily with the major corporations. The business community continues its political support for right-wing policies but if it can no longer do so through conventional neoliberal means as it did in the 1980s and 1990s or by support of authoritarian politics that arose in the 2000s, then it seems prepared to throw its support to neo-fascist politics. I use the term fascism advisedly. I would remind you that Franco, Hitler, and Mussolini all had certain relationships with the big corporations and worked very closely with the big corporations over time while at the same time developing their distinctive brand of socialism: national socialism.

I am not arguing that a move of this sort is inevitable, but I am arguing that there are warning signs that the neoliberal project is in danger and is losing its legitimacy and that those who pursue the neoliberal project among the big business community are looking for popular mechanisms of support. The global oligarchy which rules is extremely concentrated and very small. The last Oxfam report on wealth distribution, for example, said that eight individuals control as much wealth as 50 percent of the world's poorest population. Twenty years ago, they listed 340 individuals as having that amount of wealth and power. In a way, the neoliberal project has been too successful in pursuing its goal of an increasing centralization of capitalist class wealth and power.

How this wealth concentration is justified and legitimized and how it will be preserved these days are the big questions we have to face. Are we going to tolerate this putative alliance between neoliberal economics and neo-fascist political forms? Such alliances are beginning to emerge around the world in troubling ways. The Bolsonaro phenomenon in Brazil is real. We look at Duterte in the

Philippines, at Erdogan in Turkey, Orban in Hungary, and Modi in India. We look at all of these people and it is plainly a dangerous situation. The liberal establishment, Michael Bloomberg's Democratic Party, for example, is not strong enough to resist this political evolution. It will take a mass movement of opposition to counteract this neoliberal neo-fascist alliance coming to dominance. But this require that everybody knows the deep nature of the problems we face and the range of plausible answers.

6

Socialism and Freedom

The topic of freedom was raised recently when I was giving some talks in Peru. The students there were very interested in the question: "Does socialism require a surrender of individual freedom?" The right wing has managed – particularly in the United States, but also elsewhere – to appropriate the concept of freedom as its own and to use it as a weapon in class struggle against socialists who are supposedly about "un-freedom." The subservience of the individual to state control imposed by socialism or communism is something to be avoided and evaded, they said, at all costs. My reply was that we should not give up on the idea of individual freedom as being part of what an emancipatory socialist project is about. In fact, we may want to put it central rather than peripheral. The achievement of individual liberties and freedoms is, I argued, a central aim of socialist emancipatory projects. But that achievement requires collectively building a society where each one of us has adequate life chances and life possibilities to realize each one of our own potentialities.

Marx had a few interesting things to say on this topic. One of them is that "the realm of freedom begins when the realm of necessity is left behind." Freedom means nothing if you don't have enough to eat, if you are denied access to adequate healthcare, housing, transportation, education, and the like. The role of socialism is to provide those basic necessities, to fulfill those basic human needs so that then people are free to do exactly what they want. The endpoint of a socialist transition, and the endpoint of the construction of a communist society, is a world in which individual capacities and powers are liberated entirely from wants, needs, and other political and social constraints. Rather than conceding that the right wing has a monopoly over the notion of individual freedom, we need to reclaim the idea of freedom for socialism itself.

But Marx also pointed out that freedom is a double-edged sword. He has an interesting way of looking at this from the standpoint of the workers. Laborers in a capitalist society, he says, are free in a double sense. They can freely offer their labor power to whomsoever they want in the labor market. They can offer it on whatever conditions of contract they can freely negotiate. But they are at the same time un-free, because they have been "freed" from any control over or access to the means of production. They have, therefore, to surrender their labor power to the capitalist in order to live.

This constitutes their double-edged freedom. For Marx this is the central contradiction of freedom under capitalism. In the chapter on the working day in *Capital*, he puts it this way: the capitalist is free to say to the laborer, "I want to employ you at the lowest wage possible for the largest number of hours possible doing exactly the work I specify. That is what I demand of you when I hire you." And the capitalist is free to do that in a market society because, as we know, market society is about bidding about this and bidding about that. On the other hand, the worker is also free to say, "You don't have a right to make me work 14 hours a day. You don't have a right to do anything you like with my labor power, particularly if that shortens my life and endangers my health and well-being. I am only willing to do a fair day's work at a fair day's wage."

Given the nature of a market society, both the capitalist and the worker are right in terms of what they're demanding. So, says Marx, they are both equally right by the law of exchanges that dominate in the market. Between equal rights, he then says, force decides. Class struggle between capital and labor decides the issue. The outcome rests on the power relation between capital and labor which can at some point turn coercive and violent. The struggle between capital and labor is really what is involved in the determination of how long the worker must work for a day, what the wage will be, and what the conditions of labor will be like. The capitalist is free to maximize the rate of exploitation of the workers under the law of exchanges while the worker is free to resist. The collision between the two freedoms is built into capitalism on a daily basis.

This idea of freedom as a double-edged sword is very important to look at in more detail. One of the best elaborations on the topic is an essay by an economic historian called Karl Polanyi, who wrote a book called *The Great Transformation*. Now, Polanyi was not a Marxist. He may have read some Marx, but he didn't subscribe to the Marxist view of things. But he evidently thought long and hard about this question of rights and the question of freedom under capitalism. In *The Great Transformation* he says that there are good forms of freedom and bad forms of freedom. Among the bad forms of freedom that he listed were the freedoms to exploit one's fellows without limit; the freedom to make inordinate gains without commensurate service to the community; the freedom to keep technological inventions from being used for public benefit; the freedom to profit from public calamities or naturally induced calamities, some of which are secretly engineered for private advantage (an idea that Naomi Klein discusses in her work on "disaster capitalism" in *The Shock Doctrine*). But, Polanyi continues, the market economy under which these freedoms throve also produced freedoms we prize highly: freedom of conscience, freedom of speech, freedom of meeting, freedom of association, freedom to choose one's own job. While we may cherish these freedoms for their own sake – and I think many of us still do, even those of us in the Marxist camp (including me) – they are, to a large extent, byproducts of the same economy that is also responsible for the evil freedoms.

Polanyi's answer to this duality makes for some very strange reading, given the current hegemony of neoliberal thinking and the way in which freedom is presented to us by existing political power. He writes about it this way: "The passing of the market economy" – that is, getting beyond the market economy – "can become the beginning of an era of unprecedented freedom." Now, that's a pretty shocking statement – to say that the real freedom begins after we leave the market economy behind. He continues:

Juridical and actual freedom can be made more wider and more general than ever before. Regulation and control can achieve freedom not only for the few, but for all – freedom not as an appurtenance of privilege, tainted at the source, but as a prescriptive right, extending far beyond the narrow confines of the political sphere into the intimate organization of society itself. Thus, will old freedoms and civic rights be added to the fund of new freedoms generated by the leisure and security that industrial society offers to all. Such a society can afford to be both just and free.

Now, this idea of a society based upon justice and freedom, justice and liberty, seems to me to have been the political agenda of the student movement of the 1960s and the so-called '68 generation. There was a widespread demand for both justice and freedom: freedom from the coercion of the state, freedom from coercion imposed by corporate capital, freedom from market coercions but also tempered by the demand for social justice. It was in this context that I wrote my first radical book, *Social Justice and the City*. The capitalist political response to this in the 1970s was interesting. It entailed working through these demands and, in effect, saying: "We give in to you on the freedoms (though with some caveats) but you forget the justice." Giving in on the freedoms was circumscribed. It meant for the most part freedom of choice in the market. The free market and freedom from state regulation were the answers to the question of freedom. But just forget about the justice. That would be delivered by market competition, which was supposedly so organized as to assure that everyone would get their just deserts. The effect, however, was to unleash many of the evil freedoms (e.g. the exploitation of others) in the name of the virtuous freedoms.

This turn was something that Polanyi clearly recognized. The passage to the future that he envisaged is blocked by a moral obstacle, he observed, and the moral obstacle was something which he called "liberal utopianism." I think we still face the problems posed by this liberal utopianism. It's an ideology which is pervasive in the media and in political discourses. The liberal utopianism of, say, the Democratic Party is one of the things that stands in the way of the achievement of real freedom. "Planning and control," Polanyi wrote, "are being attacked as a denial of freedom. Free enterprise and private ownership are declared to be the essentials of freedom." This was what the main ideologists of the neoliberalism put forward. This is what Milton Friedman was about; this is what Hayek insisted – that the freedom of the individual from state domination can only be assured, they both said, in a society which is founded on private property rights and individual liberty in free and open markets.

"Planning and control, then, are attacked as a denial of freedom. Private ownership is declared to be the essential of freedom. No society built on any other foundation is said to deserve to be called 'free.' The freedom that regulation creates is denounced as un-freedom. The justice, liberty, and welfare it offers are decried as a camouflage of slavery."

To me, this is one of the key issues of our time. Are we going to go beyond the limited freedoms of the market and market determinations and the regulation of our lives by the laws of supply and demand, what Marx called the laws of motion of capital, or are we going to accept, as Margaret Thatcher put it, that there is no alternative? We become free of state control but slaves of the market. To this there is no alternative, beyond this there is no freedom. This is what the right wing preaches and this is what many people have come to believe.

This is the paradox of our current situation: that in the name of freedom, we've actually adopted a liberal utopian ideology which is a barrier to the achievement of real freedom. I do not think it is a world of freedom when somebody who wants to get an education has to pay an immense amount of money for it and has student debt stretching way, way into their future. What we are talking about is debt peonage; what we are talking about is debt slavery and this is something which needs to be avoided and needs to be circumscribed. We should have free education; there should be no charge for that. The same should be true of healthcare, and the same should be true of a basic provision of housing. It should also be true for the basic elements of adequate nutrition.

If we look back many decades, we went from a world in the 1960s where there was social provision of housing to one where there is none. In Britain, for example, a large proportion of the housing provision in the 1960s was in the public sector; it was social housing.

When I was growing up, that social housing was the basic provision of a necessity at a reasonably low cost. Then Margaret Thatcher came along and privatized it all, and said, basically: "You will be much freer if you own your property and you can actually become part of a property-owning democracy." And so, instead of 60 percent of the housing being in the public sector, we suddenly go to a situation where only about 20 percent – or maybe even less – of the housing is in the public sector. Housing becomes a commodity, and commodity then becomes a part of speculative activity. To the degree that it becomes a vehicle of speculation, the price of the property goes up, and you get a rising cost of housing with no actual increase in direct provision.

When I was a kid growing up, I was brought up in what might be called a respectable working-class community where there was home ownership. Most people in the working class did not have home ownership, but there was a segment of the working class that had home ownership, and I happened to be raised in a community of that kind. The house was viewed as a use value; that is, it was a place where we lived and did things – we never really discussed its exchange value. I saw some data recently that showed that the value of working-class housing showed no shift at all over a hundred years or more, up until the 1960s.

Then, in the 1960s housing started to be viewed as an exchange value rather than a use value. People started to ask, "How valuable is this? Can we improve its value? If so, how do we improve its value?" Suddenly, exchange value considerations came in. Then along came Margaret Thatcher who said, "Okay, we're going to privatize all of the social housing so everybody can participate in the housing market and start to benefit from rising exchange values." The question of housing as an exchange value started to become significant.

One of the consequences of this is that those people in the lowest elements of the population from the standpoint of income found it harder and harder and harder to find a place to live. Instead of living in very central locations where they had easy access to job and employment opportunities, they were more and more expelled from the centers of cities and from the best locations and increasingly had to commute longer and longer distances to their work and to their jobs. By the time you get to the 1990s, the house became an instrument of speculative gain. Under speculative pressures housing values increased often sharply (though also erratically). The aggregate result has been that many of the people in the lowest income levels of the population can't find a place to live. We get the production of homelessness and a crisis of affordable housing.

When I was young, in socialist Britain, there were some homeless people around, but very few. But now, if you're in London, or large cities of that kind, you find more and more homeless people on the street. In New York City we have 60,000 homeless people. A large proportion of young kids are homeless, not in the sense that you see them on the streets, but they shift from one relative or friend to another sleeping on couches – "couch surfing" it is called. This is no way to create solidarious communities.

Today we see a great deal of building going on in cities across the world. But it's speculative building; we're actually building cities for people to speculate in and not cities for people to live in. And if we create cities for investment purposes rather than for living purposes, we get the kind of situation we see in New York City where there is a major crisis of affordable housing in the midst of a housing construction boom focused on the affluent market. You need at least a million dollars to get into that market. The mass of the population is badly served in terms of its use values of housing; it has very little access to adequate use values. At the same time, we are building large, huge, high-value apartments for the ultra-rich. Bloomberg, the former mayor of New York City, had the ambition that every billionaire in the world would come and invest and have a big apartment on Park Avenue or somewhere like that. That, indeed, is what happened, so we find Arab sheikhs and billionaires from India or China or Russia, who don't live in New York; they just come here maybe once or twice a year, and that's it. This is no foundation for decent living arrangements in a decent living environment for the mass of the population.

We are building cities, building housing, in a way which provides tremendous freedom for the upper classes at the same time as it actually produces un-freedom for the rest of the population. This is what I think is meant when Marx made that famous comment: that the realm of necessity actually has to be overcome in order for the realm of freedom to be achieved. What we have right now in New York City is freedom of investment, freedom for the upper classes to choose where it is that they will live, and the mass of the population is then left with almost no choice whatsoever. This is the way in which market freedoms limit the possibilities, and from that standpoint, I think that the socialist perspective is to do as Polanyi suggests; that is, we collectivize the question of access to freedom, access to housing. We turn it away from being something which is simply in the market to being something in the public domain. Housing in the public domain is our slogan.

This is one of the basic ideas of socialism in the contemporary system – to put things in the public domain. I get some encouragement from the fact that the Labour Party in Britain – one of the few traditional parties which seems to have some vigorous democratic urgency about what it is up to – proposed that many areas in public life should be taken back from the market and brought back into the public domain – for example, transportation. If you say to anybody in Britain that private provision of transportation on the railways is producing a more efficient transport system, everybody in Britain will laugh at you. They know perfectly well what the consequences of privatization have been about. It's been a disaster. It's been a mess. It's been uncoordinated. And the same thing applies to public transportation in cities. We also see the privatization of water supply, which is supposed to be good; but, on the other hand, what we find is, of course, that water is charged for. It's a basic necessity; it should not be rendered through the market, you have to pay your water rate, and water provision has not been good.

Therefore, the Labour Party said, "Look, there are all these areas which are basic necessities for the population, and they should not be provided through the market. We're going to stop this business of student loans; we're going to stop this access to education through privatization; we're going to actually move basic necessities being provided through the public domain." There is an urge, I think, to say, "Let's take these basic necessities and take them out of the market. Let's provide them in a different way." We can do that with education, we can do that with healthcare, we can do that with housing, and we should do it with basic food supplies. In fact, there have been experiments in some Latin American countries with providing basic food supplies to lower income populations at a cut price. I don't see any reason whatsoever why we shouldn't have a basic food supply configuration for most people in the world today.

This is what it means when the realm of freedom is only possible when we have actually provided all of the basic necessities which we'll need for everyone to lead a decent, adequate life. And that is the idea of freedom which a socialist society would pursue. But we need a collective way and a collective effort to do this. Alas, the Labour Party in Britain lost the election miserably. But I firmly believe the loss came not because of its progressive program (which commanded a lot of public support) but because of the failure of the Labour Party to be decisive regarding Brexit and the inability to deal with the mass media attack upon the Party for all sorts of other supposed failings.

Finally, one point. It is often said that in order to achieve socialism, we have to surrender our individuality and we have to give up something. Well, to some degree, yes, that might be true; but there is, as Polanyi insisted, a greater freedom to be achieved when we go beyond the cruel realities of individualized market freedoms. I read Marx as saying the task is to maximize the realm of individual freedom, but that can only happen when the realm of necessity is taken care of. The task of a socialist society is not to regulate everything that goes on in society; not at all. The task of a socialist society is to make sure that all of the basic necessities are taken care of – freely provided – so that people can then do exactly what they want when they want.

It's not only that individuals have access to the resources to do it, but they also have the time to do it. Freedom – free time – real free time – is something which is absolutely crucial to the idea of a socialist society. Genuinely free time for everyone to do whatever they like is the measure of what socialism aspires to. If you ask everybody right now, "How much free time do you have?" the typical answer is "I have almost no free time whatsoever. It's all taken up with this, that, and everything else." If real freedom is a world in which we have free time to do whatever we want, then the socialist emancipatory project proposes that as central to its political mission. This is something that we can and must all work towards.

7

The Significance of China
in the World Economy

On January 2, 2019, after the stock market had closed, Apple Computer announced that it was not going to meet its sales targets, particularly in China. There was an immediate crash in Apple's stock (down by 6 percent), and the following day, the stock market that had already lost a lot of money declined by another 2.5 percent. The interesting thing about this was that it was Apple computer sales in China that triggered the problem. Apple computers are, of course, made in China, but Apple also has a significant market there. The main official explanation for the problem was that the consumer market in China was softening for a number of reasons. The main cited reason was the Trump assault upon tariffs. But the other, which came in the small print in later reporting, was stagnation in China's consumer market.

But when we look more closely, we find that Apple computers were declining in popularity and that Apple's share of the China market had been reduced to a mere 7 percent. The other 80 percent was covered by Chinese computer companies with names like Huawei, Xiaomi, Oppo, Vivo – companies that nobody had ever heard of outside of China. Most of these companies had existed only in name in 2010. There has been a huge increase in Chinese production of iPhones, computers, and the like, and that huge increase is producing at a much lower cost with much easier operating systems well adapted to Chinese uses. Many Chinese cities, and I had experienced this myself at first hand, went from a cash economy to a cashless economy in just three years, and an easily utilized Chinese-made iPhone was the instrument. I couldn't even pay for a cup of coffee with cash.

I mention this because China's presence and significance in the global economy is underrepresented in many contemporary accounts of what's going on in the world. Yet, as evidenced by the Apple case, what is happening in China is going to be determinant for global capitalist development in general. In fact, it has already been determinant, particularly since the crisis of 2007–08. Capital, and capitalism in general, was rescued from collapse into depression in 2007–08 by an expansion of the Chinese economy. We also need to come to terms with the sheer size of the Chinese economy and the rapidity of its transformation. The fact that in three years, major cities in China went from a cash economy to a cashless economy is an example.

But let us begin with the size of the Chinese economy. It is now the second largest economy in the world by conventional measures of GDP. If you take the purchasing power parity measure, which is based upon what a local currency can buy, then the Chinese economy is the largest economy in the world. If the Chinese economy flourishes, then the rest of the world flourishes. If the Chinese economy goes into a recession, then this has a tremendous impact upon the evolution of capital.

The other side of this, which is important from an anti-capitalist standpoint, is that China is still committed to its Marxist position. It is still governed by a Communist Party, and while many people will say the Communist Party is in fact a capitalist class party, it is still a nominally Communist Party in which the thoughts of Marx, Lenin, Mao, Deng Xiaoping, and now Xi Jinping, are cited as central to their ambitions. The last party congress declared that they plan to be a fully socialist economy by the year 2050. That fully socialist economy will be characterized by equality, by democracy, by a benign relationship to nature, by a cultural world of beauty and excellence. This is to be accomplished through the agency of the Communist Party. The declaration made very clear that there is no chance of democracy right now, that the continued domination of the Party was absolutely crucial, but it was the Party that was going to be the instrument for this transition to socialism with Chinese characteristics.

For those of us interested in the future of socialism, I think we need to take what is happening and planned in China seriously. We need to keep two questions in mind: to what degree does the future of socialism depend on what is happening in China, and if so, what kind of socialism will it be? The second question is: will the future of socialism worldwide be determined by what might happen in China, by this programmatic transformation of its economy towards a supposedly socialist economy with Chinese characteristics?

I think that for anybody on the left, we should pay attention to these questions because, in a sense, we live in a world where what Marx called "the coercive laws of competition" play a very important role in defining who we are. And we are very much in competition with China, and China is very much in competition with us. This competition is not only economic it is also political and cultural. This is one of the things that the Trump administration has brought into the forefront of our consciousness. We need to think about China in a more coherent way.

I'm not an expert on China. I wish I knew much more about it, I wish I knew the language. I have been there a few times, and I have read a great deal. I try to follow what's going on particularly in the financial press. But I have to say that I have not got a very clear answer to the questions that I have posed. I do not have a clear analysis of everything that is happening there. China is obviously a very complicated society, but there are nevertheless certain things that stand out for me as I seek answers to crucial questions.

The first thing is that the big transition occurred in 1978, when Deng Xiaoping and a group of young people got together, looked at the situation and in effect said: "We have to change something, and we have to change it in ways that are going to allow us to increase productivity in the economy dramatically." At that time, the Chinese economy was stagnant. And they were faced with the following situation: the World Bank in 1980 estimated that 850 million people were living under conditions of abject poverty in China and conditions were not improving. So that was one thing.

The other was that China was surrounded by countries that were developing very fast, and improving their standards of living very quickly. Japan had done so, South Korea had done so, and even more important, Taiwan, which the Chinese considered as part of China, had done so. Hong Kong, which at the time was nominally part of China, had done so, and Singapore had done so. So you had a Chinese diaspora out of the country that was flourishing, becoming pretty wealthy, and you had a stagnant economy on the Chinese mainland itself.

The Party leadership saw this was a very threatening situation, leaving aside the attacks that might come from imperialist powers directly. They realized, as Marx put it, that the world of freedom begins when the world of necessity is left behind. They had a huge gap in terms of covering the necessities of the Chinese population before they could really start to say they were a developing country. It was in that context that they decided to introduce one of those elements into the economy which was going to become critical in the years to come. They were going to force economic entities to compete with each other to increase productivity. The mechanism was to introduce market forces into the economy.

In so doing, of course, they did consult with Western economists. Milton Freedman visited there in 1980. There was a considerable revision in the way in which economics was taught in universities, so that if you go to China right now you will find very few people who have studied Marx very carefully in economics departments. Most economics departments are staffed with people who got PhDs from MIT, Stanford, and places like that. Neoclassical economics is very well understood in China, so their method of analysis of the economy started to shift, their policies started to shift. Marx's political economy is considered a branch of philosophy not economics.

This transformation was astonishingly successful. If you take any of the other countries that moved out of communism or socialism into capitalism, such as those in the ex-Soviet empire, then they all went through a period of chronic and often catastrophic economic disaster from which they have yet to fully recover. China, on the other hand, developed very rapidly. The World Bank estimated by 2014 that the 850 million people in abject poverty in 1980 had fallen to 40 million. Most recently, China plans zero poverty in the country by 2022. Whatever you may think of this, there is no question that the standard of living of people in China, their access to commodities, goods, and so on has increased very substantially. This has been an astonishing achievement. But it has not only done that. It has also developed completely new ways of living.

Daily life in China has been revolutionized through rapid urbanization. By the time you get to the 1990s, there are hundreds of cities which have more than a million inhabitants. You now see a rate of urbanization which is about 15 percent per year, and a tremendous migration of populations from rural areas into the city. There are estimates in the 1990s, for example, that something like 300 million people had actually moved from the countryside into the cities over the last ten or 15 years. By comparison, the total migration from Ireland to the United States was maybe 30 million people spread over a century. When we start to compare what has happened in China with what has happened elsewhere around the globe, then the speed of transformation and scale of transformation in China is enormous, something never ever seen before in human history.

Consider one of the crucial means by which global capitalism was saved by China from total collapse in recent times. In 2007–08, you get the global crisis. This crisis crashes the consumer market in the United States, which meant that those companies and those countries feeding the US consumer market are in recession. China, it is said, lost around 30 million jobs in 2007–08 in the export industries. There was tremendous labor unrest in China during that time. There are reports on the numbers of incidents of labor protest in China, and during that year, a lot of companies went bankrupt. Many of the companies didn't pay wages that they owed for six months. Many unemployed people were left on the streets with nothing.

There was a tremendous crisis for China. But by 2009 a survey was done by the IMF and the International Labour Organization (ILO) to answer the question: "What was the net job loss from the crash of 2007–08 across the world?" The net job loss in the United States was around 14 million people. But the net job loss in China was only 3 million. Somehow or other, China had created 27 million jobs in one and a half years. That is absolutely phenomenal. When I first saw this I said "nobody has ever heard of this before." But when I read further I found that China right throughout the 2000s was already creating 20 million jobs a year. There was a huge transformation in employment already in motion and they had simply doubled down on that to deal with the crisis.

Now, in 2007–08, they couldn't create jobs in the export industries, because the export industries were dead, and many of them were going bankrupt. So, what China did was to expand a process that had begun in the 1990s. They expanded infrastructural investments, particularly in the built environment. I have a graph I often use to illustrate this, which is the consumption of cement in China. If a lot of cement is consumed it means there is a lot of construction going on. China after 2007–08 tripled its consumption of cement to the point where between about 2009 and 2012, they consumed far more cement in two or three years than the United States consumed in one hundred years. Now, living in the United States, you know there is a lot of cement consumed, but China was consuming at an astonishing rate, and they were building almost without cease and without limit. They were building new cities, they were building new roads and highways, they built a high-speed rail network. They had zero miles of high-speed rail in 2008, by the time you get to 2014 they had around 15,000, maybe now they have around 20,000 miles of high-speed rail. All of this takes a lot of materials, so China boomed in terms of its infrastructure investment.

If you remember what happened after 2007–08, there was a proposal in the United States to say: "Look, we can put everything back to work, we have all of these bridges that are falling down, we should be investing in infrastructures." Politically, it wasn't allowed to happen because the Republicans in particular said: "We need austerity, you can't expand the budget, you can't do those things." So a politics of austerity was pursued in the United States, a politics of austerity took hold in Europe, and a politics of austerity was promoted in Japan. You have this politics of austerity in the rest of the capitalist world saying: "The crisis of 2007–08 was a debt crisis, we've got to pay off the debt, how are we going to do that? Through a politics of austerity. People have to suffer in order to retire the debt and get the economy back onto a good basis." And then you look at what that meant for countries like Greece, and you see the appalling results of that kind of politics.

The Chinese did exactly the opposite, they said: "Okay, we've got this problem, we've got all of these people milling around, there is tremendous social unrest, we have to put these people back to work, we've got to create millions of jobs and do it very fast, we're going to do it in construction. We're going to build, and build, and build. How are we going to pay for it? We don't care. We're actually going to pay for it in indebtedness, or whatever way." And the Chinese borrowed in their own currency, not in a foreign currency, and this then allowed them to get out of the crisis. Now, as they got out of the crisis, of course, if you're building like crazy, you need materials to build. One of the consequences was that all of those countries and all of those economies that were supplying raw materials like iron ore and other minerals to China came out of the crisis of 2007–08 fairly quickly. Australia, for example, provides a lot of mineral resources to China. Latin America experienced the crisis, but not as badly as you would have thought in normal circumstances. Countries like Chile were sending copper like crazy to China, the rest of Latin America was sending soybeans and minerals. That is what I mean by China saving the global economy in 2007–08.

China's astonishing expansion was critical at that time, and has been critical ever since. China's increase in GDP has actually been the most significant element in the revival of the global economy since 2007–08. But as I have indicated, a lot of it was debt financed. And the debt limit was exceeded. The second thing that happened was that China was not only using debt financing, but was having to expand its internal consumer market. They had to build the consumer capacity within the Chinese economy. Now, this is something that is important globally, because the interest of foreign capital is not only in using China as a place to produce low-cost goods, it is also an interest in China as a consumer market.

I mentioned in the beginning that the Chinese market was terribly important to Apple, even though it is no longer doing well in that market. There are some other companies that do tremendous business in China. For instance, Starbucks is reputed to have more cafes in China than it does in the United States. If Trump messes around too much with the Chinese I can just imagine them putting restrictions on Starbucks, so you may see US firms in general having a hard time doing lucrative business in China. Some US automobile firms are already running into complicated relations with the Chinese authorities. This may be one of the ways in which China can create a counter-movement to Trump's tariffs. The China market for automobiles is now the largest in the world and US companies cannot afford to be excluded.

The internal market in China is growing, but it needs to grow in a certain way. For example, if you build housing at the rate that the Chinese build housing, then people have to buy that housing or have money to invest in that housing. To do that, they need to be able to borrow. Before 2007–08, there was very little easily accessible mortgage finance in China. But when this huge building process began they had to create new instruments so that people could finance the purchase of housing. The financial sector has to be expanded to lend to companies to build housing and apartments at the same time as it has to expand to accommodate consumers to purchase the housing and the apartments. This means that financial institutions have to be strengthened to back this whole process.

In the Cultural Revolution, before 1978, banks basically did not exist in China. After 1978, banking came back into the picture very fast. Particularly after 1995 or so, the banks started to play a much more vigorous role in Chinese society. The four largest banks in the world are now Chinese. You go from a situation in 1978 when the Chinese banks don't exist to a situation where they have the four largest banks in the world – the fifth largest bank is a Japanese bank and the sixth largest bank in the world is J.P. Morgan. In the United States, we like to think we have the biggest and most powerful banks in the world, but the Chinese have four banks which are far bigger than anything we can show. These banks are lending money to developers, and they are also lending money, of course, to consumers. The Chinese economy is financializing at a very rapid rate. This is another key respect in which the Chinese economy is being transformed radically at an unprecedented speed.

The Chinese also now recognize that you cannot build a vigorous economy if the only form of industrialization you have is the low-wage, high labor content forms of production. The Chinese now plan to transform to an economy producing high-value goods by capital-intensive means. This is where the new Chinese computer companies suddenly come into the picture. Again, notice the speed with which this has happened. A lot of Chinese entrepreneurs, scientists, and engineers had training in the United States. Many of them had worked for Apple and Google and in the computer companies, like Microsoft. An interesting debate occurred within China about if they could create the equivalent of a Chinese Silicon Valley. And if so, how could they do it?

One of the big misunderstandings about China is that everybody in the West thinks of it as a highly centralized economy. It is not. It's an incredible machine in which centralization and decentralization work together. Essentially, the Party in Beijing proposes something. The rest of the country responds in a totally decentralized and localized way. People try to find their own distinctive way to respond to what it is that the central government is asking. The central government proposes, while the locality disposes. Decentralization is a very significant tool for perpetuating centralized power.

The method the Chinese use is if they have got a problem, then it gets farmed out in a certain way. All of the localities, the cities, and the regional governments are invited to help solve the problem. If one locality solves the problem, then the central government instructs everyone to adopt this model solution to the problem. This whole system means that you need local entrepreneurs who are going to be very active. It seems that the localities are very insulated from each other. They form competitive entities within the totality of the Chinese state, and they compete intensely with each other.

The mayors of a local city do not get elected, they get appointed by the Party. The average length of tenure of a mayor is three and a half years, let's say four years. So, you're a mayor for four years, and at the end of four years, you're going to be evaluated. You're in the

Party, and the Party is going to look at what you have done. At the end of four years, there is a spreadsheet that measures achievements: how much did you grow the local GDP? How did you do in terms of ensuring social harmony? I was recently told that the spreadsheet is now about forty items, when it used to be about seven or eight. But a key measure is "how much did you grow the local economy?"

As a local mayor, you have four years to grow the local economy. If you do a good job, and you grow it really well, and you maintain social harmony, then you may be offered a position elsewhere. This way, you can go up in the Party hierarchy. You may even end up in the central committee in Beijing. But, in those four years, you've got to go like gangbusters to try to make things happen. You would be free to work not only on ideas or problems coming from Beijing. You could seize upon any idea which seemed to work locally and, if successful, you might hope that Beijing would look favorably upon it and reward you. But there have been some obvious cases where the Party has disapproved and local officials have been reprimanded, demoted, or even put in jail.

A couple of entrepreneurs who had experience of Silicon Valley proposed to the City government of Beijing to create a space in the city for hi-tech innovation, and to build incubators for new electronics and hi-tech companies. Local governments can easily clear a space since all the land is state property. Beijing in just six months evicted everybody from a particular area in the city and created a space called "the avenue of the entrepreneurs." They created a new organization to facilitate the start-up of incubator spaces, and they put in all necessary support facilities. They brought together all the services you might need. Beijing was having problems of very high rents on spaces. So the government invited the start-ups rent-free. Imagine that in New York or London.

This initiative was highly successful. It became an entrepreneurial space which was extremely competitive, characterized by what they call "a copy-cat culture." There is little if zero respect for intellectual property rights in that space. If somebody had a good idea, other people would steal it immediately. So, if you have a good idea you have to act upon it very fast, because if you didn't act on it fast, somebody else would take it. This was an extremely dynamic situation. In this particular space in Beijing, companies started to develop all kinds of new phone systems, new structures for utilizing them. You would go through the different phases of innovation, diffusion, implementation in a very short space of time.

This created the equivalent of a Silicon Valley, and it was done in about three years. But it had a very different philosophy and culture than Silicon Valley. In Silicon Valley, for example, stealing other people's ideas is not good. Here is how Kai-Fu Lee in his book on *AI Superpowers: China, Silicon Valley and the New World Order* describes it:

> Silicon Valley's entrepreneurs have earned a reputation as some of the hardest working in America, passionate founders that pull all-nighters in a mad dash to get a product out, and then obsessively iterate that product while seeking the next big thing. Entrepreneurs there do indeed work hard, but I spent decades deeply embedded in both Silicon Valley and China's tech scene, working at Apple, Microsoft, and Google, before incubating and investing in dozens of Chinese start-ups. I can tell you that Silicon Valley looks down-right sluggish compared to its competitor across the Pacific. China's successful internet entrepreneurs have risen to where they are by conquering the most cut-throat competitive environment in the planet. They live in a world where speed is essential. Copying is an accepted practice, and competitors will stop at nothing to win a new market. Every day spent in China's start-up scene is a trial by fire, like a day spent as a gladiator in the Coliseum. The battles are life or death and your opponents have no scruples.

This is the world which creates these new companies, which did not exist before 2010–11, but which then suddenly swept in and took 40 percent of China's market in mobile phones almost overnight. This is the kind of world which is being constructed there. Now, this explains something to me, this copying economy, which of course is one of the things that is very upsetting to US entrepreneurs because there is no defense of intellectual property rights internally within China, and not very much respect for intellectual property rights outside of China. Lee then goes on to talk about the way in which this alternative digital universe which is being created then becomes the standard by which everybody is evaluated. I sometimes visit Nanjing. The second year I was there, I went to the local planning office to see a huge exhibition which was about creating a Silicon Valley culture in Nanjing. The central government, when they looked at what happened to the entrepreneurs in Beijing, basically turned to all of the cities in China and said: "Do this." The implication being that China is going to move into high-tech, artificial intelligence, and many other high value-added activities. This is what is now happening.

The situation is captured in the Apple story that I started with. Chinese competition in this field has in short order become so fierce, and so good, that the United States is seriously threatened. For instance, one new big company is Huawei. A chief executive officer of Huawei was arrested in Canada at the behest of the United States for trading with Iran. The United States has been fiercely attacking the company on security grounds. There is obviously something going on here which is rather more than just simply a trading with Iran kind of problem. Huawei has engaged with a great deal of innovation.

The fifth generation of communication systems – 5G – which can handle mass data is now about to be installed. Huawei has been way ahead in developing 5G network technology. Other companies can't compete technically. The United States has argued that we should not invest in this technology because it will allow the Chinese government to listen in on everybody's conversations. The network is not, it is said, secure. There can be no guarantee that this network will actually work in a way which will be insulated from utilization by the Chinese government. This is the argument the US government is making, and on that basis the United States is banning the utilization of Huawei 5G technology. Some countries have followed suit, subsequent to US pressure. Australia and New Zealand have done so, the United States is trying (unsuccessfully) to convince the

Europeans. In fact, the British have recently accepted limited application of Huawei's technology. But most of the rest of the world is taking Huawei technology. It is better quality and cheaper.

Again, notice the speed of change. In 2008 we thought of China as a country and an economy which was the workshop of the world based upon low-wage labor. It still is a very important low-wage industrial economy. But since 2008, China has suddenly moved big-time into this area, and within the space of about eight years, has positioned itself to be a major competitor in high-tech industries. If you take the ten top high-tech companies in the world, four of them are now Chinese. That was not the case in 2008. This is the Chinese model in motion. It is very fast, it is very quick, it is backed by government and has the advantage of massive scale. It has mixed in within it strong government interventions, but it's also highly decentralized so that an entrepreneurial culture has become absolutely central to what you might call the "gladiator capitalism" which is emerging in the Chinese context.

Now, I think that at this point we have to ask the question: is this the future, not of China, but is this the future of capitalism? Capitalism has historically grown usually through uneven geographical development. A place develops and becomes hegemonic. If I was giving a talk of this sort back in the 1980s we would be talking about Japan, or we would be talking about West Germany as it was at the time. These were the prime economies and everybody had to do what the Japanese were doing, so everybody started talking about "just in time" production systems, and all the rest of it. By the time you get to the 1990s, Japan has fallen into crisis, Germany is mixed up with reunification. Who is the top dog in the 1990s? Well, we have the Washington Consensus which is basically the United States emerging in the Clinton years as a growth economy with a dot-com boom. The United States reasserts its position as the top dog economy. US intellectuals announce "the end of history" and say, "everybody has to be like us, because we have got the answer to how capitalism should or should not be." Then there is the economic crash of 2001, followed by the housing bubble and then the crash of 2007–08. By then the question of who is top dog and who everybody should copy is becoming an interesting global question in a highly competitive and unstable scene. Different regional hegemons seem to be in formation. There is the China circuit, the North American circuit, and the European circuit, with Japan uneasily in the middle of a lot of this.

So, here we have a situation where the Chinese are beginning to move into the top dog position, and if they move into the top dog position, you will then ask yourself: what kind of capitalism is this going to be about? And that is where the artificial intelligence comes in, because the Chinese have decided that artificial intelligence is the future. Now, what is artificial intelligence about? Well, it's about finding a way to remove labor from the production process, and this is I think the big, big question: what is going to happen to labor? The answer to that question will tell us the degree to which the Chinese Communist Party truly believes in socialism.

8

The Geopolitics of Capitalism

I want to get into the topic of the geography and geopolitics of capital because, coming from a geographical background, I feel I always
have to insert some geography into the analysis somehow and somewhere. In order to approach this from a Marxist standpoint, it is
important to recognize that Marx started *Capital* with the argument
that a capitalist mode of production is a mode of production in
which wealth is measured, or "appears," in the form of commodities.
Capital as a book begins with the theory of the commodity. The rise
of a commodity economy and a commodity political culture has
been long in the making. Here is how Shakespeare (one of Marx's
favorite authors) sets out the transition in *The History of King John*
(Act II, Scene 1).

Mad world! Mad kings! Mad composition! ...
That smooth-faced gentleman, tickling Commodity.
Commodity, the bias of the world.
The world, who of itself is peised well,
Made to run even upon even ground
Till this advantage, this vile-drawing bias,
This sway of motion, this Commodity,
Makes it take heed from all indifferency,
From all direction, purpose, course, intent:
And this same bias, this Commodity,
This bawd, this broker, this all-changing word ...
And why rail I on this Commodity?
But for because he hath not wooed me yet:
Not that I have the power to clutch my hand
When his fair angel would salute my palm;

But for my hand, as unattempted yet,
Like a poor beggar raileth on the rich.
Well, whilst I am a beggar, I will rail
And say here is no sin but to be rich.
And being rich, my virtue then shall be
To say there is no vice but beggary
Since kings break faith upon Commodity,
Gain be my lord, for I will worship thee.

Shakespeare wrote this at that historical moment when the merchant form of capital was beginning to assert itself in Britain and Western Europe. The monetization of everything began to be very significant. Before that, people organized their thinking and their actions mainly through loyalties to kin and to family with a lot of exchanges being goods in kind. This difference between loyalty to family and obedience to monetary incentives frequently crops up in Shakespeare's plays.

This difference is registered even today. Consider the TV series *Game of Thrones*; in this modern, popular miniseries, the loyalty to family versus the pursuit of money power theme is prominently featured. But different spatialities are involved. The loyalty to family is associated with territory but money easily crosses borders. On the one hand, it's the Lannisters versus the Starks versus the Tyrells, etcetera; the people's loyalty is to a "house," to a person, or to a family. This loyalty is different from the pursuit of gold which does enter into the *Game of Thrones* through the participation of the Iron Bank. The family is located in a particular place and space and time and therefore is often defined territorially. The Starks are in the north and the Lannisters are in the south, etc. Their loyalties are embedded in a territorial structure. Wars between the families and factions are waged across those territorial structures.

In the European situation in Shakespeare's day, these wars were incoherent and episodic, engaging all manner of different alliances. This can get confusing because it is often hard to tell who's backing whom and why factions switch sides. Throughout Europe, some order was imposed on this chaos by the Treaty of Westphalia in

1648. This put an end to the long period of wars of religion, wars of ethnicity, wars between clans, wars between everybody. It basically settled on the idea that there should be something called the state, a nation state, within which there would be sovereignty. The general idea was that every state should respect the sovereignty, the integrity and the borders of every other state. This did not always hold in subsequent history, but this was a very important settlement. It clarified and stabilized the territorial structures of power across Europe. It was accompanied by the rise of a logic of political and economic power contained and corralled within this fixed territorial structure. There has been a continuous attempt since 1648 to create within each territory, under the rubric of a nation state, some kind of configuration of power, which would sustain itself internally while being able to project itself onto the world around it. This logic of power was initially built around a military presence. It also came to rest upon a superior education and a superior culture particularly of elites. Behind it lay efforts to create an ideal state. State institutions arose along with certain hierarchical structures exercising command and control over the population within the state. These institutional structures became one of the shaping and conditioning features of the rise of capitalist class power.

Marx did not deal much in his writings with these territorial structures of sovereignty and power, though he often indicated that he intended at some point to do so. As a result, there has been a long-standing and, it has to be said, generally inconclusive debate within the Marxist tradition as to how to theorize the capitalist state. Marx, however, concentrated his attention on another source of power: that which lies with control over the means of production and the capacity to engage with profitable commodity production. Ultimately, this was transformed into the power over and within the circulation and accumulation of capital. The initial measure and locus of this power lay with command over money, which historically meant gold. It was through this lens that another way of understanding arose as to what was happening in the world. Researchers frequently advise, when faced with some sort of political problem or conundrum, to "follow the money." When you follow the money, you'll find out who's really doing what behind the scenes and where the power lies. This is the capitalist form of power.

There are, then, two logics of power. One, a territorial logic that attaches to the state and its institutions and the other, a capitalist logic, which derives from the circulation and endless accumulation of capital largely through the actions of private interests. In the latter case you can aspire to immense power by becoming one of those eight billionaires that are said to control 80 percent of the world's resources. This power can be used to dominate and control others, the laborers and working classes in particular. But this power is wielded in a context where the territorial forms of power also operate. There is often a problem about how the capitalist billionaires relate to territorial state power and vice versa. The more powerful capitalists and their factions frequently try to turn the state into an agent of their own interest. But state power is more complicated than that because the state has to respond to the wants and needs of a diverse population of citizens and the billionaires might not be popular with that population. The big question is the legitimacy of who has power within the state. There is also a perpetual contest over how monetary power is exercised within the state apparatus. The question arises as how best to understand the relations between these two logics of power. To begin with, the two logics are not separate from each other. They are constantly interacting with each other. For example, an affluent class will set up international institutions to regulate what's happening in the monetary field, but regulate it in such a way as to confirm or alter the territorial logic of power and to advantage territorial elites relative to the class of cosmopolitan capitalists.

The IMF, for example, plays an important role in regulating how monetary exchanges shall occur across the globe. There are other institutions like the Bank of International Settlements in Basel, which perform similar functions. Then there is the World Bank. There are many such institutions with a great deal of power over the paths of capital accumulation. There are also many private institutions that are global in reach. One of the most powerful of them in our own society is, for example, McKinsey. The international consultancy, accounting, and law firms have a huge influence not only over legal and financial questions but they are also the source of a lot of public policy analysis. Anybody who comes to territorial power generally calls in McKinsey or one of the other big consultancy firms if they have a problem.

All of these firms typically provide neoliberal recipes for action and all of them seem to be on the same page when it comes to policy implementation. I have often fantasized with some colleagues about creating a left-wing version of McKinsey so when somebody comes into power who has real left-wing politics, they've got a consultancy organization that can provide a socialist answer to policy problems such as lack of affordable housing or how to deal with environmental degradation.

The relationship between territorial structures of power and the capitalist logic of power is something that needs careful attention. When you look at the capitalist logic of power, Marx argues that capital is value in motion. This logic of power is all about motion and everything is contingent upon its movement. There is a flow of money, a motion of commodities, a motion of production, a motion of the factors of production like labor and resources and the like. The monetary forms of power are not stationary or static but constantly in motion. One of the things that's very difficult for a state to do is to prevent, control or even contain that perpetual motion. The more static and spatially constrained forms of state power are perpetually challenged by the motion of capital.

When Mitterrand became president of France in 1981, he decided he was going to use state powers to implement a socialist program. He nationalized the banks and sought to reorient the economy to the conquest of the internal market. To do this he needed to control the movement and the potential flight of capital. Capital's response to Mitterand's program was to race out of the country as fast as possible. It did not want to operate in a world controlled by socialism. The state's response was to impose capital controls. This meant controlling and restricting the use of credit cards abroad. Back in the 1980s, credit cards were not quite as popular as they are now. But in France, the Carte Bleue, as it was called, which is in effect a Visa credit card, was very popular. People used it when they went on vacations. Mitterrand had to control the use of Carte Bleue. The population of France was absolutely outraged. Within a few months, Mitterrand realized that he could not control the flight of capital out of the country. His popularity plummeted to almost zero. He had to reverse course. He reversed the nationalization of the banks and became a good neoliberal president (like Thatcher across the Channel) thereafter. The power of capital flow disciplined the capacities of the state apparatus. The power of capital had by then become an all-powerful force regulating what happens in the global economy. It clearly had the capacity to discipline territorial power across the whole world. During the neoliberal period the state has increasingly been mobilized as an agent of monetary and capitalist class power. The bond-holders control the power of the state in their own interest.

There was a wonderful illustrative moment when Bill Clinton was elected president in 1992. This may be an apocryphal story. He had just been elected and he set out to outline his economic program. Clinton's economic advisors, most notably Robert Rubin, who came from the major investment bank Goldman Sachs, looked at him and said you can't do that economic program. And Clinton replied, "why not?" And Rubin said something like, "Wall Street won't let you." "Do you mean to say," Clinton reportedly said, "that my whole economic program, and all my prospects for re-election, are dependent on a bunch of fucking Wall Street bond traders?" And Rubin apparently said, "yes." Clinton came in promising universal healthcare and all kinds of wonderful things, and what did he give us? He gave us NAFTA. He gave us the reform of the welfare system so it became much more punitive. He gave us the reform of the criminal justice system that accelerated mass incarceration. He gave us the WTO and at the end of his term, he repealed Glass-Steagall, the last firewall of regulatory control over investment banking. In other words, he implemented a whole program that Goldman Sachs had long wanted. There have been very few moments in US history since Clinton when the Secretary of the US Treasury has not come from Goldman Sachs. This is an important indicator of the way in which the bond-holders dictate what can be done in the realm of state power.

If you say this in the United States, you are immediately accused of conspiratorial thinking. Nobody believes you. But if you go to Greece and ask the people there whether or not the government or the bond-holders control things, then you get a very different answer. If you go on to ask: "who forced all this austerity down your throats after 2011? Who's really in control here?" The answer is, of course, the bond-holders and a socialist government, Syriza, which at a crucial moment caved in to financial interests, to implement measures which were demanded by the bond-holders. And there are similar struggles going on all over Europe. In Italy right now (2019), there is a struggle because the bond-holders are essentially saying one thing, not directly but through the European institutions, and the Italian state powers (such as they are) say something completely different.

Greece's indebtedness was initially to European banks, particularly to German and French banks who had lent without restraint after 2000 or so. If Greece had declared default in 2011, that would have meant that the French and the German banks would have been right-royally screwed. The German and French governments would have had to bail them out to compensate for their losses from the Greek default. But serious pressure was put on Greece by European powers not to default. The Greeks were promised again and again they would get help from the European Union. But that did not happen. The debt owed to the banks was transferred from the private banks to the so-called Troika – the European Central Bank, the European Stabilization Fund, and the IMF. So instead of the private banks going bankrupt, the international institutions assumed the debt and insisted on payment. The Troika mandated an austerity package: Greece had to privatize state assets, sell off all public goods, assets, and lands (it was even suggested that the Parthenon should be privatized!). The state had to cut pensions and all forms of social expenditures, close hospitals, schools, and the like and people had to learn to live with almost no social supports or social services. Greece was put into this situation. If you ask the Greeks themselves "who's in control here, your government or the bond-holders?" you would get a very clear answer. This turns out to be very much the situation everywhere in the world right now.

The global situation is that accumulation of capital is dependent upon the way in which territorial governments respond to the prospects for the accumulation of capital. So what do we see? The most recent example we have in the United States is Foxconn, which says it will come to Wisconsin and open a factory of some sort provided it receives a sufficiently attractive subsidy package. Amazon likewise says to New York City, we are thinking of setting up in your city so you must provide us with all the help and all of the funds we need. Again and again, large corporations say we have all of these different places where we can go – which one of you will give us the best deal? Amazon actually announced that it was going to set up some new campus and it invited bids, sparking inter-urban and inter-state competition. It was offered a good deal in New York City but the citizens revolted and so Amazon said it would go elsewhere. In the end, some of it did come to New York City but to a different neighborhood. Foxconn negotiated with Wisconsin and the government decided they would give Foxconn $4 billion in subsidies to come and set up a factory. Foxconn is interesting because much of Foxconn's work is in China making Apple electronics but Foxconn is a Taiwanese firm. It's a Taiwanese firm with major operations in China that is now setting up in Wisconsin, provided that it is given sufficient subsidies (mainly in the form of forgoing future taxes). The calculation is that the state is offering over $200,000 for every created job. Having agreed to this, Foxconn then turns around and says "oh, by the way, we're not actually going to manufacture anything there." We're simply setting up a research campus. The Wisconsin government cannot do anything about it. The power relation between the territorial entity and the corporation has tended to favor the latter in recent times.

This does not make territories irrelevant. Many researchers came to that conclusion in the 1980s, even to the point of saying the state is now irrelevant. All the power lies elsewhere. With power moving towards big corporations and the increasing ease of geographical

mobility, small geographical differences became even more important than they were before in the drive to maximize profits. Large
corporations look for the advantages of being located in one place
rather than another. Even a small tax advantage between one place
rather than another could become decisive. This means that local
governments or even whole nations (Ireland is very good at this)
have organized their taxation arrangements to offer maximum
advantages to private corporations. This produces fierce inter-urban
and inter-regional and international competition between states to
try to attract foreign investment. This is one of the big aims of state
power right now. The result: state power becomes subservient to
private capital. So if it is not the bond-holders it is the large
monopoly corporations who are in control.

This was not the case in the 1950s and 1960s in the advanced
capitalist countries because the state, at that point, was much more
social democratic and much more powerful relative to capital. Part
of the state's mission was to guarantee well-being to the mass of its
population. It didn't always work and, yes, indeed, there were many
problems (e.g. of paternalism). Also, back in the 1960s and 1970s,
there were strong capital controls so that you couldn't move money
around the world as easily as you can now. I remember the first time
I went to the continent from England. I had to apply to the bank to
get traveler's checks. I was only allowed 40 pounds of traveler's
checks and they stamped that amount in the back of my passport. I
could not get another 40 pounds until the following year. This sort
of thing today would be unbelievable, but when I was a kid, that was
the situation. Everybody in Britain was living under a regime of
capital controls. Such controls were consistent with the Bretton-
Woods agreement of 1944 about how the international monetary
system would work. The Bretton-Woods system of international
capital controls broke down at the end of the 1960s and was
abandoned in the 1970s. After that we started to get much more
fluid movement of money capital within the world economy.

This brings us to the question of the geographical movement of
capital. Capital in the course of its motion assumes three primary
forms. The first is money. The second is as commodity. And the

third is as production activity. Which one of those forms of capital is most easily moved? It turns out it's the money form. I think of money as the butterfly form of capital. It flits around the world and wherever and whenever it sees a tempting flower to alight upon, it lands on that. And then it picks up again and flies off somewhere else. The commodity is the caterpillar form of capital. It crawls around rather slowly and is often cumbrous and hard to move (e.g. steel rods versus diamonds). The third form of capital, production, is the least mobile. Which one of those forms dominates in a particular historical period is, I think, terribly significant and in part the answer is given by how mobile the capital needs to be.

Giovanni Arrighi had an interesting argument that is relevant to this point. He said, capital reaches a point where its got real difficulties of expansion in its production form and its commodity form is getting very sluggish. When that happens, there's likely to be a push to create a more fluid financial system. He documents periodic switches of this sort throughout history. Venice and Genoa both got to a point where they became financiers in addition to commodity traders and producers. As financiers, they became much more geographically mobile and flexible in their use of money. This financialization played an important role in the movement of power and capital from the Italian city states, northward into Holland. This constituted the second hegemony within the world trading system. Merchant and finance capital focused on the Netherlands and the power of the Netherlands with Amsterdam and Antwerp and the powerful merchant cities, such as Utrecht and Bruges, being powerful centers of capital accumulation.

But this system reached its limits to produce another phase of financialization, which produced another hegemonic shift of capital concentration and centralization to Britain in the late seventeenth and eighteenth centuries. This was the capital that produced the Industrial Revolution to ground a different kind of hegemony within the world system with industrialization at home and colonies and imperial occupations abroad. This was ultimately followed by the financialized move from Britain to the United States, which became the unrivaled hegemonic center of the capitalist system after 1945.

Arrighi claimed that there were signs that the United States was beginning to reach its limits in terms of its productive capacity in the 1980s. Around this time we see a strong movement into financialization. And the big question right now is where is the finance actually going to go? It goes to wherever the production capacities are most open to fresh exploitation. And right now that happens, of course, to be China. Whether or not this means that China is destined to be the next global hegemon is an open question. Each hegemonic shift entailed a dramatic alteration of scale from the Italian city states, to the Low Countries, to Britain and ultimately to the United States. A shift of scale will be required to displace the United States and that is almost unthinkable in its implications. Arrighi thought it might now entail the rise of Asia as a conglomerate hegemonic region. In terms of population, China plus India plus Indonesia would certainly qualify but it is hard to see how any of that might work together and, if so, what the implications might be for production, consumption, social well-being, and environmental conditions.

This is one of those situations in which a financialized capitalism is very fluid in terms of which flower it is going to alight upon and where conditions are optimal for financial investment and capitalist development to occur. This is the situation we're now in. Again, it's the money form of capital, which is mainly re-territorializing capitalist structures and economic and political power in our times.

In the first part of this chapter I focused on the geographical mobilities of the different forms of capital and how a territorial logic of power organized through state apparatuses and governments contrasted with the molecular geographical flow of corporate capital engaging in commodity production and financial operations. I now want to attack this whole question from a different angle, using a theoretical construct of which I am rather fond, which is the idea (or theory) of what I call a "spatial fix."

Capital develops and as it develops, so it expands. The geography of capital is therefore about its endless expansion in and over space. Within a particular territory, the possibilities for expansion are ultimately limited by the resources, by the population, by available infrastructures, and the like. At a certain point within that territory capitalist expansion reaches a limit. Capital surpluses stack up in a particular part of the world, often accompanied by surpluses of labor. These capital surpluses need an outlet for profitable employment. So where can they go? One answer is to develop colonies. Another answer is to export capital (and in some instances also labor) to some other place in the world where the capitalist system has yet to develop. This is what I call "the spatial fix" as an answer to the over-accumulation of capital that is the inevitable product of profit seeking.

Marx has an interesting description of how this spatial fix works. The territory with surplus capital lends money to some other place in the world, which uses it to buy commodities from the capital surplus country. The destination country can use the commodities it purchases either to satisfy the wants and needs of its population (through consumerism) or to build infrastructures and operations conducive to the further development of capitalism in the destination country.

Britain, for example, had a serious surplus capital problem after 1850 or so. The internal market was satiated and there were few profitable opportunities to employ capital within Britain. Thus, Britain started to export capital. But there were different models of how to do this. One typical game it would play would be this. It would lend money to Argentina to build railroads. But all the railroad equipment would come from Britain. So British loan capital lent to Argentina would mop up the surplus productive capacity for steel and railroad equipment production in Britain. The problem of surplus productive capacity is solved, but at the same time Argentina builds railroads across the Pampas that serve to get wheat to the ports as cheaply as possible. And then cheap wheat is sold to Britain. Cheap wheat in Britain lowers the cost of bread which means industrialists can cut wages and increase profits because the reproduction costs of labor power are lower. In this way, a surplus of capital in one part of the world is used to develop an expansion of the capitalist system elsewhere at the same time as it raises profits in the originating country by lowering costs of basic consumer goods.

In the nineteenth century, the centers of capital surplus were very few and far between. They were mainly located in Britain and some parts of Western Europe. A lot of capital surplus flowed to the United States. There are two things that can happen with this surplus of capital. It can either be controlled by state power or open and fluid flowing through the market system. Here the British relationship to the rest of the world in the nineteenth century is instructive. Britain needed to expand its markets. Through the absorption of India into the British Empire, the British destroyed the Indian village textile weaving industry and replaced the products of Indian industry by imports from the textile factories of Britain. India was organized as a captive market for British industry. But India had to pay for the imported textiles somehow. How was it going to do that? Something had to be exported from India in order to be able to pay for the British textiles. India did have some exports. Tea and jute and things like that. But they weren't sufficient. So the British "persuaded" India to produce opium to send to China. The Chinese market for opium was forced open by military/naval action (the so-called "Opium Wars"). China had to pay for the opium with silver which first went to India before going from India to Britain to pay for the textiles. Rosa Luxemburg outlines this in her book on British imperialism, *The Accumulation of Capital*. In this case, the spatial fix to the problem of surplus productive capacity in the British textile industry rested on the destruction of the Indian apparel industry, the transformation of the Indian market into a captive export market for British product, and then the creation of these other forms of production and commodity trading such as the opium trade, which brought in enough silver to pay for the textiles.

But this spatial fix also required something else. And this "something else" entailed the production of adequate physical infrastructures. Marx has, again, some very interesting things to say about India in this regard. One of the ways in which the Indian market could be unified and made more accessible to foreign domination was through investment in transportation and communications. Britain built the railroads in India. If you go to India these days, you will see an elaborate Victorian railway station in the center of

Mumbai, which is a sign of this British colonial activity. So, again, the export of surplus productive capacity to some other part of the world to build infrastructures required that this other part of the world have some means to pay for it. Foreign capital could lend the money to build the infrastructures which would yield a rate of return to the foreign capital through their use. And if the infrastructures improved the productivity in India or the ability in India to produce and sell through the market, then everyone could benefit. Here again we see a form of the spatial fix at work. The utilization of India as a source of raw materials, as a source of extraction of monetary wealth and as a market was foundational for Britain to deal with its tendency to produce capital surpluses.

But there is another form of spatial fix through capital export which was most clearly represented by the United States. Surplus British capital came to the United States because there was an open territory for development as a result of the genocide of the native population. But in the United States, it was not used simply to create a market. Some of that went on. But it was also used by US-based entrepreneurs to create an alternative center of capital accumulation. It was invested in productive activity, rather than organized to satisfy consumerism. British capital played a very important role in funding not only the creation of an alternative market but the creation of a whole new center of capital accumulation within the United States. As it takes off in the United States, the demand for machinery and other means of production increases both in the United States and in Britain and Europe. And that is putting a lot of demand into the global market, some of which is going to be met by the expansion of British production for the US market. But this process serves to create a territorial rival in the field of capitalist commodity production. The United States, at some point, developed its own form of capital accumulation which was bound to come into competition with British and European production. The United States competes with Britain and ultimately defeats Britain for hegemonic position in global capitalism through competition. So, in a sense, Britain played a key role in financing the agent of its own demise. This, too, is a form of the spatial fix.

But the spatial fix plays a very important role in relationship to crisis formation because it also entails long-term, temporal as well as spatial displacements. Take the case of investment in railroads in the United States. This form of investment is long term. It's not as if you get a rate of return within six months. If there's going to be a rate of return, it's going to be a long time in the future and because over that long term the productivity of the US economy is going to rise. But this is going to be over a period of 10, 15, 20 years. This is a very long-term investment. And long-term investment means appeal to some sort of credit system which allows you to mobilize money power over a long-term time horizon. This entails the use of what Marx called "fictitious capital" (a transferrable and marketable monetary claim on something that does not yet exist) to eventually build the new infrastructures. These infrastructures then become the basis for an alternative form of accumulation and alternative dynamics in the circulation of capital. Such systems have an interesting history. Spatial fixes of this sort have been going on at increasing speed in the global economy since 1945 but particularly since 1970 or so. Surpluses of capital from the United States and from other parts of the world have been deployed to create alternative production systems in other open spaces. The alternative production systems have not been primarily about creating new markets.

I have argued (and this is controversial) that as far as nineteenth-century Britain was concerned, the Indian venture was less profitable for British industry than the US venture, because colonial power in India suppressed the inherent dynamism of capitalism (the "animal spirits" of the entrepreneurs) in favor of constructing a passive consumer market. The British aimed to prevent a rival capitalist production system developing in India. They wanted to keep India in their pockets as a market. But this holds back the dynamism of capital. It ultimately checks the growth and continual expansion of the market. So the Indian solution became less and less profitable in the long run for British enterprise. Whereas in the United States, Britain did not control matters, it could not control the dynamism that would, on the one hand, continuously expand the spatial fix available through the development of the US market at the same time as it would lead the United States ultimately to out-compete Britain in the geopolitical struggle for hegemony.

After 1945, there was a real problem in the global economy. The fear was the return to 1930s depression conditions but this time with a huge increase in productive capacity associated with the war economy and a lot of military personnel returning home. And the US policy makers actually understood something important. The United States would benefit from decolonization. Colonial possessions should be taken out of the control of Britain or France or Holland. They should not be held as captive markets by imperial powers. The United States did not have as many captive markets and so, in its own interest, it demanded and commanded that all those markets be opened up. The United States figured it could colonize those markets just as easily as Britain and France could but through a global free trade system.

Decolonizing and opening up the world to alternative structures of development would help absorb US capital surpluses. This was the genius of the Marshall Plan. But the Marshall Plan was not simply about trying to use Europe as a convenient sink for surplus commodities from the United States. It was also about rebuilding capital and sites of capital accumulation all over the world to expand the world market dramatically. To the degree that surplus capital moved to Japan and to Europe, so it led the revitalization and revival of the Japanese and the European economies. The period from 1945 until 1970 or so was one of astonishing growth in the global economy and much of that depended upon the creation of these alternative centers of capital growth and accumulation in Japan and in Western Europe. By the 1980s, these alternative areas of accumulation started to out-compete the United States on the world stage. So the United States suddenly found itself in a situation in which it had helped create its own rivals. If I was giving this talk back in the 1980s, I would be talking about Japan and West Germany as being hegemonic in terms of global capitalism. They were the ones that were really racing ahead. And the United States had encouraged that because it was to the benefit of the United States to encourage it, particularly in the context of the Cold War with the Soviets and the prospect of a communist alternative as it was emerging in China. But then the United States was faced with the problem of how does it confront West Germany's and Japan's explosive growth. The US answer was to create a rules-based world order where we can all compete and we can all benefit from open trade with each other. The United States saw globalization and free trade in open markets as the solution. They were also convinced they could win under this rules-based system (in part because it was constructed to advantage US capital).

This was the neoliberal order of free trade, of systematic reduction of tariff barriers, the creation of a global financial system that facilitated the easy movement of both capital and commodities from one part of the world to another. The creation of new technologies of transport and communications and so on helped a great deal. A lot of things went into this. But one of the consequences was the development of multiple alternative centers of capital accumulation. Japan, for example, develops very strongly during the 1960s only to find itself with huge quantities of surplus capital at the end of the 1970s. And what is it going to do with it? The Japanese explore spatial fixes through the export of capital. They also start to "colonize" the US consumer market. The Japanese "invasion" of the US economy then followed. They bought the Rockefeller Center. They got into Hollywood, buying Columbia Pictures. Surplus capital is flowing from Japan back into the United States. But it also expands around the rest of the world, even assumes a mini-imperialist posture in many emerging markets such as in Latin America. Shortly afterwards, we see similar sequences going on throughout the rest of Asia. South Korea develops, not initially as a free market economy but under military dictatorship. But the United States encourages South Korea to develop for one very simple geopolitical reason: the containment of communism. The Soviet Union and China posed a threat. In order to contain communist expansionism, you needed a prosperous capitalist, pro-capitalist South Korea. The United States supported the development of the Korean economy and facilitated technology transfer and offered favorable access to US markets. But by the end of the 1970s, South Korea is generating surplus capital with its incredible productive apparatus. So what does it do? It seeks a spatial fix. It sets up automobile production in the United States and takes over some US electronics firms while colonizing US markets and organizing production in other emerging markets. Surplus capital surges out of South Korea around the end of the 1970s. Suddenly sub-contracting firms appear in Central America and Africa run by the Koreans. The labor practices and the human rights practices of the Koreans are pretty brutal.

But before you know it, the same sequence occurs in Taiwan. The United States supports Taiwan because it wants a prosperous economic development in Taiwan to make sure that it remains in the US orbit rather being absorbed back into communist China. So Taiwanese industry starts to become very important. In about 1982, the capital surplus problem emerges and there suddenly appears a stream of capital exports from Taiwan. Where's it going? It's going all around the world but a lot is going into China which has just opened up to capitalist development. This was the moment when Foxconn, which is now one of the biggest conglomerates in the world, started to move into China. South Korean producers moved into China also as did the Japanese. But Taiwan moved massively. So they all started to move production into China. Chinese development, then, is very much based upon Taiwanese, Japanese, South Korean, and, of course, Hong Kong capital after 1978. Hong Kong was a very interesting case. Before China opened up, Hong Kong's textile and apparel industry had already defeated and out-competed the British textile industry, which was already being de-industrialized. Manchester textiles and apparel factories could not compete with Hong Kong textile products. Hong Kong capital wanted to expand but lacked the labor, the resources, and the market within their territory. Then China suddenly opened up and Shenzhen opened. Hong Kong capital flew into China to take advantage of a mass of cheap labor power. Chinese industrialization in the 1970s and 1980s was a result of all of these capital imports coming from Hong Kong, Taiwan, South Korea, and Japan.

The result was the creation of an incredible productive economy within China. And what did that economy do? It starts to defeat its competition. What happens to Japan? The Japanese economy has been in a slump since about 1990. Taiwan has been struggling even as Foxconn, which is a Taiwanese firm, employs 1.5 million people in China. But now Foxconn has productive capacity in Latin America and Africa. It is even going to Wisconsin. Here is the spatial fix in motion. Capital is perpetually moving from one place to another.

It is now China's turn to confront the problem of what to do with surplus capital. Maybe it is a coincidence or maybe it is not. But in 2008, everything in China seems to have changed direction. This was the year of a huge crisis in global capitalism. China's major consumer market in the United States crashed and exports to the United States fell dramatically. But in 2008, for the first time, foreign direct investment into China was overtaken by China's export of capital abroad. After that, capital exports soared, way ahead of capital imports. China becomes an aggressive net exporter of capital. Most of the export takes the form of commercial credit rather than as direct investment in production. China is supplying commercial credit to East Africa to absorb China's surplus product (e.g. steel rails). In 2000, the map of China's capital exports was essentially blank. But by 2015, Chinese surplus capital is all over the place. The whole world is being caught up in China's search for a spatial fix for China's surplus capital. The Chinese start to orchestrate this around something called the "Belt and Road Initiative," which is a geopolitical expansion plan in which surplus capital from China is allocated to rebuild the transport and communications connectivity of the Eurasian continent, with offshoots across Africa and into Latin America. Geopolitical strategies of this sort have had a long-standing history.

Halford Mackinder was a professor of geography at the University of Oxford where I taught for seven years (1987–93) holding the Halford Mackinder professorship of geography. Halford Mackinder was a reactionary right-wing imperialist, writing in the first half of the twentieth century. He was also a geopolitical thinker who came up with the following formulation. He said whoever controls the Heartland of Central Europe controls the World Island of Eurasia and whoever controls the World Island controls the world. The Chinese have been thinking about their geopolitical position and power for at least ten centuries. They have read Mackinder. The United States also has its distinctive geopolitical theory and history. But the US muse was Alfred Thayer Mahan, who wrote about the role of sea power in history during the 1890s. Mackinder emphasized land power and Mahan sea power. Halford Mackinder was most influential back in the 1920s but continued to write up until World War II. In the 1920s and 1930s, there arose a whole school of German geopolitical thinking: *geopolitik*. They argued that states are a bit like organisms. As such they need to feed freely on adequate access to resources (such as oil) and define their own living space. The theory of *Lebensraum*, associated with the German geopolitician Haushofer, was absolutely crucial to Nazi ideology about the path towards world domination. The Nazi expansion into Eastern Europe (and the oil fields of Romania) in the 1930s appealed to the necessity of the German state acquiring living space and controlling the world island. The struggle for world domination centered on control over the Heartland of Central Europe as Mackinder had defined it. Control over the Heartland created the path towards world domination. Hence, the invasion of Czechoslovakia and then Poland.

What we're seeing right now through China's Belt and Road project is an expansion of China's geopolitical influence in Central Asia. The spatial fix to China's capital surplus problem is being converted into a geopolitical project in which Central Asia is being absorbed into China's sphere of influence by infrastructural investments. It is interesting that the United States organizes much of its global power through sea power and there is a serious conflict emerging between China and the United States in the South China Sea, but China also emphasizes land power in Central Asia where the United States finds it difficult to exert much geopolitical influence. China is beginning to assert almost complete control over what's going on in Central Asia and the United States is not in a position to contest China's influence. But China's Belt and Road project is much larger than this. It is now playing a very large role in

Africa which in just a few years since 2008 has become deeply indebted to Chinese loans to build infrastructures (such as railroads throughout East Africa). Capitalist expansion in Africa is becoming marked (e.g. in Ethiopia and Sudan). Most Chinese investment in Africa (and Latin America) takes the form of commercial loans rather than as foreign direct investment (though there is some of that with respect to mineral resources such as copper in Zambia). The Chinese are engaging in the classic tactic of lending money to countries to buy up surplus Chinese product (steel, transport equipment, and cement) in the same way that Britain self-interestedly sustained development in Argentina in the nineteenth century.

But there is also the geopolitical angle. I don't think Mackinder was right, but the Chinese maybe think he's got a point and that the control over Central Asia is a critical geopolitical project in its own right. This would explain their brutal approach to the Muslim Uighurs in western China. If they're thinking in these terms, then they're going to use their surplus cement and steel production to build railroads right throughout Central Asia and ultimately to Europe. The first trains now are going from China to London. And it takes two or three weeks or so instead of six weeks or more by sea. The Chinese figure that they will be able to radically reduce the time it takes to get from China into Europe by having a fast-track railroad network through Central Asia. This is what they are building. Western financial commentators often portray this is as economically wasteful investment. It can't be profitable. It will probably not be profitable in the short run. But in the long run, it's actually going to reconfigure, geopolitically, how the whole world is structured. The Chinese project is almost certainly geopolitical rather than primarily economic. So it's no accident that the Chinese, who for many years did not contest the United States anywhere, are contesting US power in the South China Sea. But they have also got a terrain, Central Asia, where they're not contesting anybody. Russia does not contest the Chinese project. Indeed, the Russia-Chinese alliance seems to get stronger by the year. The United States has no capacity to do anything much in Central Asia. And it's interesting. When I was in China I was advised several times against saying anything negative about Russia since there is plainly an alliance of interests in Central Asia and beyond. Both countries are supporting Venezuela in the face of repeated US attempts to overthrow the Maduro government either by direct coup attempts, sanctions, or the fomentation of internal unrest. You're beginning to see the emergence of a shadowy geopolitical divide around the world that may soon become an active contest. But notice how this Belt and Road project also converges with the problem of finding a spatial fix to dispose of surplus capital and surplus productive capacity.

Capital is bound to a 3 percent compound rate of growth forever, which means a compounding rate of reorganization of the global geography of capital and capital accumulation. What we're beginning to see is that these rolling spatial fixes, from the United States to Japan, from Japan to China, from China into Central Asia and Africa – this is a geopolitical manifestation of the logic of compounding growth of capital. Geographically we've got to be very careful. This is the kind of thing that gave rise in the last century to two world wars. Geopolitical rivalries were involved both times. I'm not arguing that there's bound to be a world war or anything of that kind. I'm just saying that the role of geopolitical rivalries and theories needs to be analyzed very carefully. Given all the current stresses, particularly in the Middle East, it would be foolish to ignore them. When the search for spatial fixes for overaccumulating capital fuses with geopolitical rivalries as happened in the 1930s, then it is time to step back and take great care not to fall headlong into the maelstrom of global wars. The geopolitics of the spatial fix has to be a focus of serious study.

9

The Growth Syndrome

The first time I taught Marx's *Capital* was back in 1970. I taught it every year after that for many, many years. But this year (2019) I have been doing Volume 1 live again after a lengthy break. It's always interesting to come back to Marx's text. The circumstances in 1970 were very different from those of 2019. Consider, for example, how I viewed the long chapter about machinery and modern industry. For many years, Marx argued, capital struggled to develop a technology appropriate to its own nature. This technology – the factory system – differed substantially from feudal technologies based on the labor skills and primitive forms of organization that characterized the "manufacturing" period which lasted from 1650 up until the Industrial Revolution of the late eighteenth century.

When I taught all this in 1970, we went through the chapter on the manufacturing period as if it was merely of historical interest. The really important stuff was in the next chapter on the factory system. Marx provided us with a fantastic (even if rather lengthy!) account of how the factory system was set up and how it spread and with what social consequences. The factory system was not just one machine; it was about a system of machines, machines producing machines, with immense implications for how labor was used, positioned and abused in production. Generic forms of technology like the steam engine could be applied in all sorts of different areas. The materials Marx culled from the factory inspectors' reports furnished a living testimonial to the revolutionary nature and the painful travails experienced in the transition to the industrial form of labor.

But this time through, I suddenly thought: a lot of young people in the United States these days probably wouldn't know much about factories. They probably wouldn't know an actual factory worker let alone a unionized factory laborer. In the 1970s most households would have had some contact with and knowledge of the world of factory labor.

In the United States, the factory system has largely disappeared. But what has replaced it? What really intrigued me this time though was that a lot of the things being said in the chapter on manufacturing actually resonated with contemporary realities. Precarious labor, for example. The constant shifting of scales and divisions of labor. The attempts by those who command skills to monopolize them and procure for themselves a privileged position in the workforce. A battle was being waged by capital against such monopolizable skills and there were constant attempts by capital to re-proletarianize the labor process and the laborers so that the privilege that attached to their monopoly skills disappears. In the eighteenth century it was particular tools which conferred privileges but in our day it is skills with computer algorithms and other such information technologies.

This is strange, I thought, because Marx sometimes lapses into teleological thinking about human evolution, suggesting that there is a forward progressive movement that is unfolding inexorably towards some pre-determined future of communism. Factory labor will ultimately replace everything else, he seemed to imply, at least within capitalism, if not beyond.

It feels rather odd when it looks as if things are moving backwards. I had always had reservations about teleological readings of Marx. My sense was that he was not deeply committed to it, though it often crops up. Even in his time, it was pretty clear that there were many labor processes not of the factory sort, and that these persisted even in the periods and places where factory labor was at its most developed. The thesis that factory labor was destined to drive out all other forms of labor seemed to be forever incomplete. Take, for instance, the Japanese automobile industry in the 1980s. Very large corporations using factory labor existed at one level assembling the automobiles. But on the other hand, when you looked at the supply of all the parts to the auto industry, it was being done in many small workshops employing skilled labor with multiple echoes of the manufacturing system.

I'd always thought that maybe Marx is not quite right in suggesting that the factory system would drive out all these other forms of labor. This was also true of the changing labor processes I was studying in Second Empire Paris. Instead of seeing large factories taking over – there were, of course, some that did – what you saw was a proliferation in specific and specialized divisions of labor in many sectors organized on artisan lines. For instance, around 1850 Paris had a significant artificial flower industry, and by the time you get to about 1855, they've started to specialize. In 1850, one workshop would make artificial roses and another artificial daisies and so on. By the time you get to the 1860s, you find workshops specializing in petal production, some of them are specializing in making stems, and still others making leaves while somewhere somebody is putting them all together. In Second Empire Paris, you don't see a move towards factory labor, but an increasing dispersal of the division of labor across these many small artisan enterprises which were becoming more decentralized rather than more centralized as would be the case with the factory system.

My conclusion has been that the industrial form has been perpetually in transformation and that capital has always had a choice between different kinds of labor processes and different forms of organization. Capital goes for the form which is most appropriate and most amenable to the particular style of exploitation in which it is engaged. One of the reasons why you get the decentralization of labor processes in the neoliberal period is because workers in the factories were rather well organized and unionized. One way for capital to avoid that is to adopt an alternative decentralized labor process, which could not be so easily organized by the laborers.

All of this is going through my mind when I'm teaching these two chapters on the manufacturing and the factory systems. I think about how capital moves from one kind of structure of exploitation to another, and that if labor becomes very strongly empowered as it had in the eighteenth century through the monopolization of certain skills, then capital would try to break that power. The factory system devalued and deskilled labor power, but by the time you get to 1970, exactly the opposite problem arises. The labor employed in the large factories is well organized and is exercising considerable power vis-à-vis capital, so the best thing capital could do was go for another labor system that was decentralized in which labor couldn't challenge capital in the same way. It is partly for this reason that we have seen so much dispersal and decentralization of industrial activity, accompanied by horizontal and networked forms of organization rather than the hierarchical forms of organization that formerly prevailed. I find it very interesting that that is the predominant move that capital made, but it also turns out that this is the dominant move that has occurred in left organizing. Left organizing has become more decentralized and horizontal. Like capital, it has become anti-hierarchical, against the political forms that arose in response to the Fordist labor process and factory system.

All of this points to the very interesting way in which when you read *Capital* critically (as you should) ideas come to you about what's going on around you and why in the here and now. Questions get posed, and these questions are critical to ask today even though the answers may be different. Let me take a seemingly small example from a reading of Marx's text to illustrate this point.

Economists, policy makers, and politicians along with the financial press frequently cite the rate of growth as a key measure of the health and well-being of the economy. To stimulate an increasing rate of growth is frequently cited as a key policy objective. But there's another aspect to growth which is significant and important, the significance of which is largely neglected. This is the mass of the growth. How much absolute growth has there been and what are we going to do with the mass that is produced?

The other day I was reading my favorite financial journal, the *Financial Times*, and it summarized a Bank of England report on whether quantitative easing had contributed to inequality. What it showed was on average, the bottom 10 percent of the population in Britain received about £3,000 in aggregate between 2006–08 and 2012–14, whereas the very rich, the top 10 percent received on average £325,000 over that period. You might immediately infer from this that quantitative easing benefited the wealthy more than it did the poor. This is a widespread claim. Even the then British prime minister, Theresa May, subscribed to it. The report, however, denied this was so. The £3,000 that the bottom 10 percent received was a greater proportionate increase than the £325,000 of the top 10 percent. Quantitative easing proportionately benefited the poor more than it benefited the rich. The problem, the authors of the report concluded, is that people don't understand how to read economic information properly. People should concentrate on rates of change not on absolute numbers.

My point here is that £3,000 over six years is less than ten pounds a week for the least well-off. That does not substantially increase anybody's economic and political power. It is a fairly trivial amount: the quantity was largely irrelevant to their lives, whereas for the top 10 percent, £325,000 is quite relevant although, given the amount of money they've already got stashed away, they might also consider it trivial. But it is a significant contribution to the mass of the wealth which they control and to the mass of the wealth that they can use for political, economic, and other purposes to sustain their power. While the rate of change may have been lower, the absolute effect was much more significant for the top 10 percent.

A low rate on a large sum produces a very large mass. Put it this way: would you rather have a 10 percent rate of return on $100 or a 5 percent rate of return on $10 million? Clearly, the 5 percent rate of return is going to produce a much larger mass and this can be the source of much greater inequality. Over six years the bottom 10 percent could get themselves three extra cups of coffee a week while the top 10 percent would have enough to buy a studio apartment in Manhattan. The report's authors are right to say we need to read the data right. But we need to do this critically. The report's recommendation disguises the unacceptable increase in inequality by proposing a measure of rates rather than masses which makes it appear as if the impacts are acceptable.

This question becomes crucially significant in certain contexts. Take, for example, the issue of global warming. While it's clearly important that we intervene in the rate of increase of carbon emissions, which in itself poses important political questions, there is another set of political questions which are posed by the already existing mass of greenhouse gases (carbon dioxide, methane, and so on) in the atmosphere. That, it seems to me, is the immediate, severe problem that we should be looking at. Focusing on the rate of increase does not help with that. There are situations in which the mass of greenhouse gases becomes much more significant.

In fact, there is very little discussion of the existing mass and its consequences in the public media and this is a serious problem. Interestingly, amongst Marxist economists, there's also a fetishization of rates and very little consideration of the significance of the mass. This comes out in the famous discussion that Marx had about the falling rate of profit in Volume III of *Capital*. The theory of the falling rate of profit has framed a lot of Marxist thinking about crisis formation. There is, it is said, a tendency for the rate of profit to fall embedded within the capitalist dynamic. It arises out of the application of labor-saving innovations in the labor process through competition between individual capitalist firms for what Marx called relative surplus value. Firms with a superior technology can sell at the social average price while producing at below the social average cost. This produces an excess profit, and competition for that excess profit drives technological innovation. Once I have a superior technology, I get the extra profit and my competitors respond by innovating to trump my superior technology by getting a superior technology of their own. Part of the dynamism of capital is powered by this sort of competition for technological advantage. But the competition for technological advantage is constantly economizing on labor and raising the productivity of labor, and by raising the productivity of labor, you are, of course, reducing the value that is produced. Competition for relative surplus value produces a class consequence which is that there's less value and surplus value to go around. The result is a tendency for the rate of profit to fall.

This argument is laid out in Volume III of *Capital* and the text that most of us use is the one Engels edited. While it is important to acknowledge the tremendous work that Engels did, he could not do it without shaping some things in ways which may or may not have been consistent with Marx's intent. Marx wrote about the problem of the falling rate of profit in one long chapter as a continuous argument. He starts by laying out the falling rate of profit argument and he seems very pleased with himself. He has solved a problem that had mystified the classical political economists. But then he seems to say, "Well, this is a starting point that enables us to look at some more very general questions." Engels divided Marx's single chapter into three. The first is called "The Falling Rate of Profit," the second is "Countervailing Influences," and the third is "Contradictions in the Law." Engels made it seem as if the law was the central thing and everything else entailed modifications of the law in practice. You come out thinking that the law is foundational and the rest is secondary.

But when you read the notebooks, Marx seems to be saying something else. And this "something else" turns out to be fascinating. Far from being a countervailing force, the increasing mass of profit is viewed as a joint product. Marx puts it this way,

> Despite the enormous decline in the general rate of profit, the number of workers employed by capital, i.e. the absolute mass of labor set in motion by it, hence the absolute mass of the surplus labor absorbed, hence the mass of surplus value it produces, hence the absolute magnitude or mass of the profit produced by it, that mass can therefore grow and progressively so, despite the progressive fall in the rate of profit. This not only can but must be the case of the basis for the capitalist mode of production.

This is far from being a countervailing force. "The same laws," says Marx, "produce both a growing absolute mass of profit, which the social capital appropriates, and a falling rate of profit."

This poses Marx with a problem. "How then should we present this double-edged law?" he asks. We are confronted with a "double-edged law" of a decline in the rate of profit coupled with the simultaneous increase in the absolute mass of profit arising from the same process. "The same reasons," says Marx, "that produce an absolute decline in surplus value and hence profit bring about a growth in the mass of the surplus labor, surplus value, and therefore profit produced and appropriated by the social capital. How," he says, "can this be explained? What is it dependent on? On what conditions are involved in this apparent contradiction?" These are the central questions he poses.

Here we have a central contradiction. While the rate of profit may be falling, the mass of profit may be rising. This tells us something very critical about the nature of a capitalist mode of production. The implications are important. A recent article in the *Financial Times* commented on the significance of the falling rate of growth in China over the last six months of 2018 which produced nervous responses in financial markets. This expectation was that this would produce serious global problems. A recession in China might produce a global recession, maybe even a depression. But, it seems the Chinese were not concerned. When asked why not, the answer was that the Chinese were primarily concerned with labor absorption. They needed to create 10 million urban jobs a year, which is a lot compared to, say, 3 million in the United States. But the Chinese could easily generate 10 million jobs on a much lower rate of growth in 2018 than was possible back in the 1990s when they were growing at 12 percent or more. It was hard if not impossible then to generate 10 million jobs, but it was easy in 2018 with a 6 percent rate of growth, because they had a sufficiently large base upon which a lower rate of growth could produce the jobs they needed. So they were not bothered by the lower rate of growth at all. They did not need to stimulate the growth rate to meet their policy objective of creating 10 million new urban jobs.

The larger the economy, the lower the growth rate has to be to produce new jobs or new demand. But that is not how policy makers think or talk. "We've got to have 4 percent growth," Trump said when he took power, bragging that "we'll soon have 4 percent growth." It did not happen and we have had low growth rates during his presidency, but the question is whether or not that really matters. Many of the things which are required and needed in society can be supplied with only a very modest rate of growth. A high rate of growth would pose another kind of problem. For example, if the output of automobiles doubles because the productivity in the auto industry doubles, then there will be twice the number of automobiles on the street consuming twice as much gasoline and twice as much of a prospect for traffic jams. If that happened globally, what would that do to global warming and all the rest of it? In other words, we have to take very seriously the question of the mass. We can take it in a positive way, as in the Chinese case of absorbing labor, or in the negative way, which would be contributing to global warming by increasing the mass of automobilization. Even though the growth rate is low, if the auto industry is very large and if that low growth rate applies to the automobile industry, that means a vast number of new cars on the road, which increases the mass of carbon emissions, which makes the problem of the existing mass of greenhouse emissions worse and worse.

I conclude: the relationship between rates and masses has to be taken seriously. It is too often neglected in the literature. When it is mentioned its significance is too often downplayed. The rates matter but what happens with the mass is just collateral. When it does crop up, as in the Bank of England report, it turns out that emphasizing rates instead of masses is exculpatory for the upper classes. Watch out for class bias in the way in which economists and the media report on the world! In the Bank of England report the bottom 1 percent are invited to celebrate their extra three cups of coffee a week with their $3,000 and are urged to appreciate it as worth far more than buying a small studio for $325,000.

10

The Erosion of Consumer Choices

One of the delightful things to do with Marx is to riff on his sometimes quaintly expressed Victorian ideas in relation to contemporary circumstances and to connect his theorizing with what's going on around us in the here and now. One of the themes that comes up very strongly in the chapter on machinery in Volume I of *Capital* is that the autonomy of the worker is taken away by the factory system. The pre-capitalist skilled worker artisans were in control of their tools. They had a certain power because their contribution to production was the skill in using their tool. This was a "free gift" of labor to capital. On the other hand, it was one of those gifts which is a poisoned chalice. Capital has to accept that the laborer is autonomous because it is the laborer who has the skill. If the laborers "downed tools" then the capitalist was lost, and if the workers did not want to do work in a particular way they didn't do it.

However, what happens with the machine is that the skill is located inside of the machine. The autonomy in terms of the speed of the process is now located outside the purview of the laborer. We get the Charlie Chaplin *Modern Times* picture of an automaton in which the laborer becomes, as Marx calls it, an appendage of the machine. The laborer has to do what the machine wants the laborer to do at the speed set by an external power.

This thesis of the erosion of the autonomy of the worker is well documented in the history of capital. This leads me to think about the changing autonomy of the consumer. How autonomous are we in terms of our consumer choices? In what degree have we all actually become appendages of the capitalist consumer production machine? In effect you could rewrite Marx's chapter about the machine to talk about contemporary consumerism. This came to me in a big way the other day when for the first time I walked around this new area in New York City called Hudson Yards. This is touted as the biggest real estate development in the United States, perhaps even in the world, though frankly I don't think it goes anywhere near what has been going on in China. The incredible thing about Hudson Yards is that you enter into it and there's a shopping mall. My reaction was: "Why does New York need another shopping mall?" This shopping mall is built with beautiful materials, large areas through which you can walk though there's no space to sit down unless you go into one of the coffee bars, restaurants or whatever. It's a very barren environment. Beautiful in its own way, architecturally beautiful some might say. But, at the same time, it seems empty not necessarily of people but of any real meaning. Which leads me to ask "how did this monstrosity, Hudson Yards, get built?"

It's interesting that since its virtual completion last month, the commentary on it has not been positive at all. Mainstream art critics and architects and so on have been very critical. It represents the expenditure of a vast amount of money and resources in terms of the glass and the marble and all the rest of it, all to make a space which is frankly not very inviting to be in. I suspect most people feel that. So, there is talk now of "well we have to get more greenery in it. We've got to do more gardening. We've got to make it more user friendly." They just opened a public space called the Shed, which is supposed to be a space of spectacle. But again, it becomes transparently obvious that the role of the Shed is to create as many spectacles as possible so that people come into the space and then afterwards will wander into the mall and maybe eat something or will buy something. It's all about the manipulation of one's needs and desires. It's all about building something in the image of capital.

This was how Marx talked about the factory system. He said the factory system was not built to lighten the load of labor. In fact, he starts off the chapter on machinery by commenting on how is it that John Stuart Mill could not understand why it was that machinery, which should lighten the load of labor, actually ended up making the labor process more and more oppressive. Well, we can say the same thing about Hudson Yards. Here is a situation in which capital is building something, which to a casual observer should be about improving the qualities of life of the population, and at the same time all it really does is to present a symbolic presentation of the nature of what contemporary capital is about. It's a symbolic intervention not a real intervention. There are some people who are going to live there but when you ask about housing prices it's certainly not anything about affordable housing. Most of the housing is very high quality for, again, the top 1 percent of the top 10 percent. You then say to yourself: "What would have happened if all of the resources that went into building this place had been actually put into the creation of affordable housing which New York desperately needs? What kind of city would we be living in?" Furthermore, what would have happened had this gargantuan effort been oriented to creating the possibility of consumer choice in terms of, for instance, different ways of life, ways of being?

It will be interesting to see if the site gets occupied by people and "civilized" by actually turning it into a place where something vibrant can go on, like Washington Square, for example, which is a public space where when the sun comes out the musicians appear and all kinds of people on skateboards, people playing cards, with the chess and checker players in the corner. There's a whole way of life there and it'll be interesting to see if anything like that transpires within the space of Hudson Yards. That can happen in spite of the awful architecture if people will it. In Paris, for example, the Pompidou Centre, an art center, is not a bad building, but it has an awful forecourt, which is the most forbidding and boring piece of architecture you can possibly imagine. But somehow or other people get into it and turn it into a space which is vibrant and alive. This depends, however, on the authorities tolerating certain degrees of freedom within the public spaces, such that they can be freely appropriated by different people doing different things. In this way the space might actually become more interesting and livable. In other words, the designers built a space in the hope that somebody would come and render it interesting. I hope that the somebody that comes to Hudson Yards will civilize it and turn it into something radically different. All too often, however, the private interests that now manage such space forbid the interesting craziness that makes places interesting in the name of security and social control.

This takes me back to this whole question about the nature and qualities of daily life under capital. Marx had held that free time is one of the big indicators of an adequate society. Marx indicated that what we should aspire to is what he called "the realm of freedom" and that realm of freedom, he said, begins when the realm of necessity is left behind. So, a good society is one where the realm of necessity is covered; everybody has enough food and enough clothing and enough housing and enough employment and enough access, if need be, to lead an adequate life. Then, after that, everything is free time. People do what they like, in whatever spaces that they like. In other words, what we're looking at here is the idea that there's going to be some sort of autonomy of how people use their time, how people consume their time. But the possibility of that autonomy has been steadily eroded by the invasion of capital into everyday life. Capital takes away the autonomy of our time and makes it impossible for large segments of the population to leave the realm of necessity behind. In fact, the largest segment of the population is struggling hard to get access to basic necessities, which means that they have a very restricted capacity and time for freedom of expression. Cities at their best are cities where there is a great deal of social autonomy of social groups to do what they want, how they want to do it. We again and again see the technologies and the capacities for an autonomous and free form of life eroded, taken away, removed.

This is one of the sad parts of contemporary life. More and more time is taken up, more and more consumer choice is controlled. Consider something like the internet, which has a very interesting history. What began in the military was taken up through an artistic peer-to-peer creative system in which all sorts of innovations were going on, powered by creative individuals very often in partnerships or in conversation with each other. At that time, the internet seemed to be a vehicle for real social advancement and social communication, social production and even in some instances social revolution. But within a few years, that process got monopolized and increasingly managed as a business model. The capitalist business model takes over so we get the Facebooks, we get the Googles, we get the Amazons, all of which are essentially monopolizing the qualities of daily life and inducing all sorts of forms of consumerism, which seems to me to be lacking soul. This is what Hudson Yards feels like and it is no surprise that Amazon, which was rebuffed from locating in Queens, is taking up a lot of the vacant space in Hudson Yards. Amazon and Hudson Yards deserve each other but there is nothing in it for us. It looks great (shimmering and shiny) from a distance – a shining city on a hill. It looks an Oz from afar, but when you get close up there's nothing much happening there and there's nothing much that happens emotionally to the population that circulates within it. Again, I don't want to say that it's impossible that the space cannot be converted into something different. Populations do take control of their social spaces and give them a flavor and they make much of what a city is about when capital merely fosters non-autonomous forms of consumerism.

Marx doesn't spend too much time talking about the consumer side of things. But this consumerism goes back to earlier talk, which is that as the mass of capital exponentially increases, so the question arises where's the market for that rising mass? And how is that mass going to be absorbed through consumerism? As we increase the total amount of commodities, then obviously there must be larger and larger populations to consume those commodities. But they must have the money to buy those commodities. All of this means that society has to be structured in some way around not only dealing with the tendency towards a falling rate of profit but to deal with the difficulty of realizing the value of an increasing mass and that increasing mass is now becoming more and more problematic. I frequently cite the case of cement consumption in China where in two years China consumed 45 percent more cement than the United States consumed in a hundred years. This is an example of an increasing mass of production and consumption of cement through a massive urbanization project designed to counteract the recession of 2007–08 in China's export industries. Which poses the problem: if the mass continues to increase as it has in cement production and consumption, then we're going to encounter serious problems for consumers as well as for the environment.

This is one of the key difficulties we're facing over global warming and other environmental problems right now. The increasing mass of commodities is associated with an increasing mass of waste. There is now a sudden burst of concern to ban plastic bags and other plastic products because their waste mass is now circulating in the oceans, producing dreadful examples such as finding a dead whale with its stomach full of plastic bags. The increasing mass of plastics production, consumption, and waste disposal is something that has to be looked at. The global demand for basic resources has also surged. The output of copper, of lithium, of iron ore has leapt upwards largely in response to China's astonishing urbanization. Even under conditions of falling rates of profit the mass of commodities in circulation is still rising at a compound rate. The increasing mass of mineral extractions resulting from wasteful urbanization (like Hudson Yards) has to be understood as something necessary for the reproduction of capital and the sustaining of capital accumulation. But to what degree is this extractivism necessary for the reproduction of a way of life of the people? And what kind of way of life is it going to be? I have often commented in the past that while there's a lot of discussion about what kind of cities we want to build, the real question is what kind of people do we want to be? It is the answer to the latter question that should define what kind of city we would build. I don't want to be the kind of person who would want to live in Hudson Yards without a good deal of prior civilizing influence, which is very hard to imagine. It is hard to imagine those high rises being taken over by the homeless, by punk rock groups, or by feminist communes, all of which might make the social environment rather more interesting.

The increasing mass of output in general and mass consumerism in particular has typically been regarded as a positive feature in capital's human history, albeit accompanied by a grumpy undercurrent of discontent with some of the qualities of daily life that are associated with the stresses of living in a hard-driving and competitive consumer society. I think we should approach the question of consumerism from a totally different perspective. The endless and compounding growth syndrome of contemporary consumerism which parallels the endless accumulation of capital needs critical evaluation and response. We should, for example, be thinking more creatively of decreasing and controlling the mass of resources we are extracting from the bowels of the earth to feed the contemporary compensatory consumerism that is so critical to the endless accumulation of capital. This is one of the big social and political tasks now facing us. As many people are now pointing out in the climate case, it is easy to recognize that things once they reach a certain mass become difficult if not impossible to control. But the true point then is that thinking in terms of controlling the rate of carbon emissions becomes less and less relevant because the mass is already large enough to do extraordinary damage.

In all of these questions the issue of the mass versus the rate is crucially significant. But none of these issues can be dealt with in isolation. The endless expansion of capital imposes a certain lifestyle on the mass of the population. But expansion dictates changes in lifestyle and the rate of turnover in lifetime also accelerates. These are the kinds of lifestyle shifts which attach to the consumerist principles and labor processes of endless accumulation. The subjective motivations and desires for instant gratification are part of the totality of relations which support and confirm the core principles of neoliberal capitalism.

Speed-up, for example, is integral to a capitalist mode of production. It's one of the ways in which I can get ahead of you in terms of the output that I have and my competitiveness. If I move faster than you, I win. Therefore, there is a tremendous emphasis upon speeding things up and the result of that is that most of us have to live much faster lives in terms of everything; we have to consume faster, adapt faster, and work faster. Relaxed, slow consumption becomes an unrealizable fetish. People like to think an alternative society can be constructed by returning to the use of slow and local foods. I like the idea of slow foods but, on the other hand, that's not how most people are going to be able to live and that's not going to be a revolutionary consumer movement by any means. But it does at least pose the question of how the speed at which a society is working, the way in which wants, needs and desires are changing so that instantaneous satisfactions are involved, where spectacle displaces real objects as objects of consumption. The advantage of spectacles is that they are instantaneously over. There may well be an attempt to validate Hudson Yards by organizing spectacles in the Shed and various other places. Maybe they can find a museum to come there, to try to culturally validate the rest of the environment. The analysis of capital has to think about rate, mass, speed, and the totality of relations. Rate, mass, and speed affect consumerism too and the effect is to define a particular lifestyle, which for many people has become alienating and alien even as it proffers surface satisfactions and instantaneous gratifications. This is a situation in which discontents with the qualities of daily life can easily fester and grow.

11

Primitive or Original Accumulation

Part Eight of *Capital* deals with what Marx calls primitive or original accumulation, which is the story of how capital came to be and how it came to power. One of the things I like about reading *Capital* is that Marx changes his writing style depending upon the topics he's covering. There are some passages which are very lyrical, some passages are densely theoretical, some passages which are factual historical accounts, while others are dry as dust accounting of how much of this equals that. But the final session on primitive accumulation is composed of short, sharp and brutal chapters. It is almost as if Marx is trying to emphasize through his writing style the brutality and the violence through which capital came to be what it is.

The story that Marx tells of the origins of capital is one which went against then prevailing bourgeois opinion and accounts. The political economists of the time presented the story of how capital began as a virtuous story. There were some people who were careful and thoughtful, abstemious and responsible, who looked to the future and were capable of deferring gratifications. Then there were those who were profligate and who chose to spend their time in riotous living. The virtuous people became the entrepreneurs who deferred gratification, who saved, accumulated and looked to the future. The profligate individuals were left with the only possibility of making a living; which was to offer their labor power to the frugal capitalists who took responsibility for how it might be fruitfully put to work. The other story with which we're now more familiar but which was also around in Marx's time was that capital derived from Christian virtues, an interpretation that Max Weber later on turned into a major text, *The Protestant Ethic and the Origins of Capitalism*. An ethical Protestantism and Quaker abstinence came to the rescue of a failing feudal economic system. Quaker virtue, deferred gratification, careful management of money, entrepreneurial skills, and loyalty to family supported by private property lay at the root of the rise of capitalism. Marx didn't have Weber's version of the story, but there were plenty of accounts that emphasized the nature of Christianity, Martin Luther, and Quaker forbearance for Marx to dwell upon. Marx takes on all such accounts and dismisses them. Things did not happen that way. The reality was that capital came into being in, he says, "letters of blood and fire." It was a violent, brutal process; the usurpation of a former system of governance, a usurpation of power relations, the robbery, thievery, violence, fraudulence, the misappropriation of state power, the utilization of almost every kind of criminal means that you could possibly imagine.

This is the story that Marx wants to tell. Maybe he overdoes it a bit, but on the other hand, when we look back we see there was a good deal of what he was talking about going on throughout this history. He dismisses the religious story out of hand as total hypocrisy. If you want to see what the religious folk really did, just look at the way in which the Christian parish was organized, the treatment of the poor in the poorhouses, the orphanages, and that. They built the prisons and set up an incarceration politics (that has lasted to this day). The violent repression of vagrants and the abuse of human dignity accompanied the way in which Christianity dealt with problems of unemployment and poverty.

But the main story Marx wants to tell is the violent means by which the mass of the population was deprived of access to the means of production – most notably the land – and deprived of the possibility of reproducing their daily life outside of selling their labor power as a commodity to the nascent capitalists. This violent expropriation, and this violent reorganization of the social order was, as far as Marx was concerned, the original sin of what capital was about. And I think it is interesting to see the way in which he articulates this notion of an original sin. Because there are some thinkers, for instance Derrida, who would say that any social order, as it comes into being, bears the marks of its violent origins, and that social order can never expunge that history. The violence of its origins continually haunts it and returns, again, and again, and again to haunt it. This is a very good moment to look at the return of many of these violent forms of expropriation, expulsions, evictions, and the like which Marx describes as being present in the very origins of capitalism. It turns out that a lot of this sort of thing is going on all around us today. The fraudulence, and the lying, the mystifications to cover over the egregious appropriation which is going on by the wealthy and the powerful, preying on the vulnerable and the small groups in the population. This is an interesting moment to contemplate how we are currently being haunted by the violence of primitive accumulation.

Marx argues that the feudal order was undermined in a number of very distinctive ways. It was undermined partly by merchant capitalism based on buying cheap and selling dear or directly appropriating products from vulnerable populations powerless to resist the military and financial power of the merchants. The order was also undermined by usury. The money lenders did a good business of dispossessing the lands. So if you put together the money lender and the merchant capitalist, together they undermined feudal power. This opened up the possibility for the accumulation and concentration of money capital in very few hands. This could then be used to try to dispossess the mass of the population of whatever productive assets they controlled. Marx's story of primitive accumulation is in the end about the formation of the working class that has no means of existence or subsistence apart from selling its labor power in labor markets.

This is the secret that Marx wishes to reveal to us through various historical stages. It occurs of course first on the land, so you get the appropriation of the land, the enclosure of the land as commons, the imposition of private property on the land; and the gradual assembly of the land through the despoliation of the Ecclesiastical estates, the taking away and the privatization of state (or royal) ownership right to the land. This privatization produced a class of landed capitalists whose main task was to separate workers from the land so that they were forced out into the streets. What this meant, Marx argues, is a collapse of a social order that had been based upon access to the commons. So, one of the big movements that we see is the enclosure of the commons which is actually a legal process. Marx emphasizes the way in which illegal processes of expropriation eventually become legal processes of expropriation. The state commanded by capital passes laws to expropriate populations and privatize access to the land. Industrial capitalists arise in a different way. They take landed property and the existence of wage labor as their basis but take money power, and start to use it to make more money. This is the originary moment of capital.

This is a remarkable story that Marx tells in *Capital*. And he tells it in various ways. But one of the things that is very striking about it is the tremendous hypocrisy upon which this system is founded. And the hypocrisy really lies in this: that, on the one hand, liberal theory takes the view that private property arises when individuals mix their labor with the land and assert their unchallengeable right to the product of their own labor. But workers employed by capital do not have a right to the product of their own labor. That product belongs to capital. And workers do not have a right, either, to control the labor process because the labor process is designed by capital. The theory of liberal rights proposed by John Locke turns out to be completely perverted – turned on its head – by what happens in the seventeenth and eighteenth centuries as society begins to move towards a more capitalist social order based on wage labor.

The reason I think this is important is to ask the question: to what degree are the processes of primitive accumulation that Marx describes still with us? Marx sometimes seems to make it seem that once upon a time capital was riddled with these illegal violent processes. But, once capital had arisen and formally been constituted, then all that earlier illegality can be done away with and we're left with a society where, as Marx puts it, the subtle economy of decision-making through an economic system precludes violent expropriations and the rule of law takes over. So you get the impression from the first part of Marx's *Capital* that there is essentially a peaceful and legal market process; that market exchange is well established, that the equalization of the rate of profit is well established, that private property rights are well established, and so on. The free market system is presumed to work in a perfected rather utopian way. In the first few chapters of *Capital* Marx does take up the utopian visions of the classical political economy of Adam Smith and Ricardo. He says, in effect, let's accept their utopian vision and try to figure out the theory of how capital works on the basis of free market exchange, a legal system based on private property rights, and the like. So, you get the impression that, once upon a time, there was a violent confrontation which led to the rise of capital. But then afterwards, capital settled down and became a legal system, and everything was being worked out according to the laws of motion of capital accumulation. What Marx shows is that this system does not operate to the benefit of all (as Adam Smith claimed) but that it privileges the rich capitalists vis-à-vis the poor workers. But this was a legal process and, therefore, violence, and expropriations, and expulsions, and so forth were no longer necessary.

But if we look at the way in which society is being organized today, we see a great deal of violent expropriation going on, and a great deal of violence and coercion in relationship to the employment of labor. We are surrounded by a daily violence actually occurring in society. It appears as if the original sin of capital perpetually returns to haunt us. In our own times, this is becoming a crucial question: how to confront what in effect is the illegality of capital? Unfortunately, it is not the case that the theory of capital proposed by utopian classical political economy prevails. It is no longer the case, if it ever was, that capitalism can be construed as a peaceful, lawful, and non-coercive system. In fact, what we're dealing with here is not only the continuation but the resurrection of systems of violent expropriation that occurred in the past. We live with a form of capital based not upon the equality of exchange but a certain violence of expropriation and dispossession.

There has been some controversy about the degree to which the techniques and practices of primitive accumulation have actually continued throughout the long history of capitalism. A couple of important thinkers have argued that you cannot envisage a society that would actually be stabilized without the continuation of some of these practices. This is particularly the case with Hannah Arendt, and it is also the case with Rosa Luxemburg. Rosa Luxemburg actually went out of her way to say that Marx's account of the continuity of capitalist production is missing out on something. In her view, the expansion of the system which is required for capital accumulation depended upon the continuity of practices of primitive accumulation within the dynamic of capitalism. The only way in which capital can continue is by having a place outside of the dynamics of capitalism upon which capital accumulation can feed. This outside was given through colonial and imperialist practices. The expansion of capital depended upon primitive accumulation occurring on the margins of a capitalist society, and, Luxemburg argued, this is a permanent feature of what capitalism is about. She was saying, in effect, that imperialism is a necessary feature of capitalism, that primitive accumulation on the periphery is necessary to the survival of capital. When the periphery is totally absorbed and there is no place to go, then that would signal the end of capitalism. But meanwhile, she said, there is a real difference between understanding the dynamics of capital as a smoothly working and law-like system and the rough and tumble of primitive accumulation which is going on largely in the periphery. The absorption of areas of the periphery into the capitalist system was always going to be based upon violent appropriations and expropriations, and the violence of imperialist interventions.

This thesis is I think an interesting one to look into. There are passages in Marx's writings where even he seems to accept that something of the sort that Luxemburg describes would go on in practice. He recognizes, for example, that the expansion of the system requires an expansion of access to raw materials as well as an expansion in the market. And when this occurs he immediately says well, actually, when we look at it tactically, this is what Britain was doing in India, which became the big market for the expansion of the Lancashire cotton industry. In order for that to happen the textile industry indigenously set up in India had to be destroyed, and that was part of what British power was about – to destroy the Indian textile industry in such a way that Indians would have to consume Lancashire cotton goods. So, the market was taken care of by the opening of the Indian market through the destruction of the indigenous industrial capacity. But then India needed to have some way to pay for all of those cotton goods which were coming, and that then led to the orchestration of much of Indian production around the production of raw materials. So raw cotton, hemp, jute, and the like became export productions. However, as Luxemburg pointed out, these were not really sufficient to cover the total value of the cotton that was being imported. So India needed some other way to pay for it and here we get into the kind of, again, violence of primitive accumulation; because as Luxemburg points out, India in fact was forced by the British to start to grow opium in large quantities and then opium was taken to China and forced upon China through the Opium Wars. The Chinese did not want opium, but they were forced. Shanghai was forced open as a treaty port through which opium could be sold to the Chinese in large quantities. That opium was paid for by silver, which the Chinese had in abundance. So, in effect, Chinese silver then flowed to India, and then from India back to Britain.

What Luxemburg describes is an imperial system which is about primitive accumulation going on in the periphery and that will continue indefinitely until all of the periphery is absorbed within the capitalist dynamic; in which case capital would not be able to find an adequate market to itself. So this story is of how imperialism is the perpetuation of primitive accumulation on the periphery – and actually to this day we will still find the sorts of things that Marx was talking about going on in the periphery. For example, the mobilization of the Chinese peasantry into global capitalist production, after 1980 or so, is a classic case of primitive accumulation of the sort that Marx describes back in the seventeenth and eighteenth centuries. Similarly, the dispossession of the peasantry in India and the increasing wage labor structures in that country, and the destruction of peasant forms of organization all around the world suggest that the primitive accumulation that Marx was talking about back then has continued being a feature of a capitalist society. But again, Marx's theory of primitive accumulation is primarily geared not so much to market questions and raw material questions – it was about the formation of a global wage labor force. And I think it's significant that the global wage labor force has increased by about 1 billion people since 1980 or so. Primitive accumulation in that classic sense still remains with us.

There is some credence to be given to the Luxemburg question: what happens when the whole of the world has been organized internally within capitalism, and there is no external space for primitive accumulation to go on? In which case we will need, I think, an alternative form parallel to primitive accumulation, which is going to allow for the stabilization of the system and that is what I will be talking about next.

12

Accumulation by Dispossession

I taught a seminar some time ago with my good friend Giovanni Arrighi, who was always seeking to understand the deep shifts in global structures of capital accumulation. We were ranging across the myriad processes of capital accumulation to be found in contemporary capitalism. At some point or other I recall saying: "Look, we're not only dealing with capital accumulation based on the exploitation of living labor in production in the way that Marx describes in Volume 1 in *Capital.* We also need to consider practices of accumulation based upon dispossession pure and simple." Giovanni's response was to ask if I meant to say: "we have to think about accumulation by dispossession?" and I said: "Yes I think we have to look at that." Since then I have often been writing about accumulation by dispossession as a form of accumulation that parallels the exploitation of living labor in production.

When I talk about accumulation by dispossession I am not talking about primitive accumulation. The latter forces people off the land, encloses the commons, and leads to the creation of a wage labor force. I'm talking instead about the way that already accumulated wealth is being appropriated or stolen away by certain sectors of capital without any regard for investing in production. This can occur in a number of different ways. I argue that contemporary capitalism is heavily and increasingly dependent upon accumulation by dispossession as opposed to accumulation through exploitation of living labor in production. What do I mean by this? For example, at a certain point in *Capital* Marx examines the increasing centralization of capital. This entails that capital steals and consolidates assets from small producers who have been driven out of business. Mergers and acquisitions are big business these days. Big capital takes over the small fish, as it were, gobbles them up and starts to expand its power and its mass simply by way of takeovers of other capitals. There are "laws" of centralization of capital. The large capitalist corporations take over the smaller to create a quasi-monopolistic situation in which the large capitalist corporation dominates all else and charges monopoly prices.

If you look at something like the rise of Google, for example, how many small operations did Google take over in its expansion to the point where it now is this major corporation? This is the way that Silicon Valley works; entrepreneurs develop small apps and set up small personal companies. At some point or other, they're bought out by the big capital and they become part of a vast conglomerate. Corporations can accumulate not by employing labor but by taking over the assets of others and asset stripping. The credit system, Marx observes, becomes one of the major vehicles for the centralization of capital. Leveraged buy-outs become common. There are all sorts of strategies to facilitate the ease of buy-outs and takeovers. If the flow of liquidity is cut to some sector of the economy and firms find it difficult if not impossible to roll over their debt, then they may be forced into bankruptcy even though the business is sound. Banks and financiers can buy up the businesses and make a huge profit when liquidity is restored. This is what happened in the crisis in East and Southeast Asia in 1997–98.

Something like this happened during the housing crisis in the United States. A lot of people found themselves forced, in some instances illegally it turns out, to surrender the asset value of their home through foreclosure. Owners could not pay their mortgages and a vast number of houses had to be sold off at cheap foreclosed prices. In steps a private equity company like Blackstone to buy up the foreclosed houses at fire-sale prices. Blackstone in short order becomes the largest landlord in the country if not in the world. It now owns thousands and thousands of houses, which it rents out at a high rate of profit. As the housing market recovers and depending upon which market you're in – if you're in San Francisco and New York it recovered fairly fast, in other places it didn't – then you can sell them off at a vast profit. This is a very large segment of the economy, which is run on the basis of an accumulation process that has nothing to do with production. It is all about profiting upon the trading of asset values. But in this case it entails the trading of asset values under conditions in which the asset values are forced into devaluation at a certain historical moment by mechanisms in the market. The assets are subsequently revalued and it is the private equity companies that can capitalize on the revaluation.

This is a mode of accumulation which has nothing to do with production. When you look at it very carefully, you see that a lot of wealth in society is being captured and traded in this way. This means that the accumulation of capital is occurring through the upward revaluation of asset values. Accumulation is no longer tied to production, it rests on rigged trading upon asset values. Now, there are other ways in which we will see this process occurring. For example, if there is a part of town which is beginning to look like it's going to go up in quality we get the famous gentrification process in which low-income populations are expelled or evicted from the space. How is that done? Some of the means are legal, some shady and some downright illegal. Landlords, of course, have wonderful ways to try to get tenants out of their buildings. In the 1970s there was this strategy of burning down buildings to get the insurance and then clear the way for new up-scale development – "the Bronx is burning" was a famous statement one evening on the radio of New York City. These processes of eviction are becoming significant in urban areas throughout the capitalist world. But evicted populations have to live somewhere, usually way out on the remote urban periphery.

This sounds a bit like what Marx called primitive accumulation on the land except that it is not happening to create wage labor but to liberate spaces so that capital can come in and rebuild in a certain area, re-gentrify through a strategy of accumulation through urban-ization. When we look at something like this again it's accumulation by dispossession. People are dispossessed of their rights, of their access to good areas of the city to live in. They're forced out to live on the margins where maybe they have long commutes to get to work. And so again and again and again we will see evictions and expulsions going on. We will see similar things going on back again upon the land. There is a process of what is called "land grabbing." This is going on all over Africa and throughout Latin America. Capital is looking for good places to invest in, "Look, the future lies upon control over land and over the assets on the land, like raw materials and mineral resources and productive capacity of the land." Big capital starts to monopolize and more and more wealth gets concentrated in the hands of the rentiers rather than in the hands of the direct producers.

There is another way in which we start to see accumulation by dispossession occurring. People employed in the United States often have had healthcare and pension rights included in their employment contracts. These rights are a terribly important but threatened feature of contemporary society, particularly in the advanced capitalist world. We are now seeing some of these issues being raised even in countries like China. Pension rights are a claim upon a future income, supposedly guaranteed, based upon certain contributions people have made to their pension funds. However, many corporations find themselves in a situation where the obligations of the pension funds or in healthcare are far too much to be really continually funded over time. So, we've seen major corporations trying to shed their obligations. The major airlines have been good at this. United Airlines declares bankruptcy. American Airlines declares bankruptcy. That doesn't mean they stop flying. They go into Chapter 11 or whatever it is and that allows them to renegotiate all of their obligations under the supervision of a judge. They typically say: "We can only resume our operations by getting rid of our past obligations." And the judge says: "Well, what do you mean by that?" The answer is: "We need to get rid of our pension and healthcare obligations." In effect, the company reneges upon both, and people find they've lost their pension rights and they don't have their pension anymore. In the United States, there is a pension insurance fund, which will say: "Well, if United Airlines gives up its pension system and American Airlines gives it up then the state will pick it up." But the state usually picks it up not according to the value that people were expecting. Somebody working for American Airlines might expect to get $80,000 a year in the way of pensions but the pension fund only pays $40,000 a year, which is very difficult to live on for many people. The cancellation of pension rights becomes one important way to enhance accumulation for the capitalists at the expense of pensioners. This is what happened to many people in Greece. I have a colleague who retired there three years ago and only last month did he get the first payment of his pension. He spent three years without any payment whatsoever because the state pension had not been responsibly invested and funded. There's currently a big problem over pension rights all around the world. Big capital is accumulating on the basis of not paying for the pension rights that were offered to employees in the past.

All of these forms of accumulation are with us right now. These are not the same as those which existed when Marx was writing about the origins of capital. They are not like primitive accumulation. They concern values that have already been created and distributed under capital but are being redistributed from the mass of the population to augment the huge asset wealth within the increasingly centralized corporations and the top 10 percent of the population. We need to take accumulation by dispossession seriously. It has become one of the primary mechanisms by which capital is currently being reproduced. Accumulation by dispossession has always been there, of course, and it has always been significant. It has never gone away. Since Marx was writing about primitive accumulation in the seventeenth- and eighteenth-century capital, there were elements of accumulation by dispossession already in place and it has continued from its origins in those days until now. But since the 1970s in particular we've had more and more accumulation shifting towards dispossession at the expense of the creation of value through the employment and exploitation of labor in production. This raises interesting questions as to the nature of the capitalist society in which we currently exist. To what degree do we have to organize struggle against accumulation by dispossession? There are, of course, widespread anti-gentrification struggles in which populations seek to prevent their displacement and eviction from valued locations. You will find struggles against the loss of pension and healthcare rights. There are struggles against land grabbing which parallel what Marx talked about in the seventeenth and eighteenth centuries when state power was frequently mobilized by the affluent classes to dispossess the rest of the population. We see the expansion and diversification of the many forms of dispossession in our own times. If you look, for example, at the last reform of the tax code and tax law in the United States, what you'll see is a redistribution of wealth and power through taxation arrangements and a dispossession of certain pre-existing rights under the tax code. Flows of value are being channeled more and more to the corporations and more and more to the affluent classes at the expense of everyone else. So the contemporary tax code is a vehicle for accumulation by dispossession.

There are many techniques of dispossession. It would be important to have at hand a complete study on accumulation by dispossession in the current situation and the various mechanisms that exist for that dispossession to occur. This is a moment when the original sin that came with the origins of capitalism is coming home to roost. Primitive accumulation was built upon violence, lies, fraud, cheating, and the like. But if you look at what happened in the housing markets in the United States in 2007–08, so much of it was based upon the illegal dispossession of populations through violence, fraud and the promulgation of a certain narrative of conspiracy and lies (such as blaming the victim) which form the primary means by which capitalist class and its accompanying forms of political power now work. Accumulation by dispossession is a vital aspect of how our current economy is working. And it is, of course, generating a great deal in the way of protests. A seismic shift is occurring in our economy such that growth is now being channeled into accumulation by dispossession rather than towards the more classic means of exploitation and appropriation of surplus value through an organized labor process.

One common point between primitive accumulation and accumulation by dispossession lies in the vast wave of privatization of state and common properties that has occurred in recent times. When Margaret Thatcher came to power she immediately set out to privatize not only as much of the social housing as she could but also the provision of water, transportation and all manner of other public assets including all the state-owned enterprises. In almost all cases the public assets were sold off at a discounted value which permitted private entities to capitalize upon the privatization for their own financial benefit. The looting of the public treasury proceeded apace. Distressed entities, such as the Greek state during its crisis years, were forced to privatize all manner of state-owned assets in return for financial support. In the Greek case, there was even a suggestion that the Parthenon should be sold off and privatized in order to stabilize the finances of the debt-encumbered state.

Merchant capital then re-emerges as a major power center (relative to industrial production capital) armed with distinctive mechanisms for the appropriation of wealth. A company like Google is partly involved in the design of new vehicles for production, but most of what Google is about is appropriation through market mechanisms. It's a massive merchant capitalist operation. Apple has also become hugely important through merchant capitalist practices of appropriation in the market rather than through the organization of productive capacity at the point of production. Industrial capitalism has, in a way, become increasingly subservient to merchant capitalism and to rentier forms of capitalism. The mechanisms by which rentier capitalism and merchant capitalism work are more and more about appropriation and accumulation by dispossession than the organization of production and the exploitation of living labor in production. This is the kind of capitalist society we've moved towards. It's the one which is not going to be tamed by classical techniques of left organizing. It has to be tamed by a completely different political apparatus and project and animated by different forms of political protest than is currently the case.

13

Production and Realization[1]

Anti-capitalist struggle exists at the point of production; at the point of realization in the market; and around questions of social reproduction, not only the social reproduction of labor power but also the social reproduction of whole ways of life. I want here to take up the question of production and realization. The classic way of thinking about this in Marxist theory is to think of the factory as a site of exploitation. The factory is the site of collective labor which is set up and organized and dominated by capital, and within which value is produced and reproduced, along with surplus value. This has been the centerpiece of a lot of thinking. But what happens when factories disappear? In advanced capitalist economies like the United States and Europe, we've been through a period of de-industrialization, in which the factory has become less and less significant. This then poses an interesting question for us right now: where is the working class and who constitutes the working class? Let me first suggest something which is a little bit heterodox: maybe we should take out the term "class" at the moment and just say "working people." The reason I suggest we do this is because "working class" usually has a connotation of a certain kind of labor situation, whereas "working people" broadens the question and allows us to reconstitute a different idea of who the working class is and what the working class might do and what their powers might be in the current conjuncture.

De-industrialization after 1970 or so abolished a mass of blue-collar jobs. Take the United States and Britain, the two cases I know best. In both instances, a lot of the job losses were due to

---

1. Note: This was composed before the closures that came with the coronavirus.

technological change. The estimates are that about 60 percent of the job losses have been due to technological change over the last 30 or 40 years. The remainder has mainly been due to off-shoring, that is, taking the low-wage jobs and going to China, or Mexico, or wherever. But with the technological change, what we see is the reduction of labor forces from very large masses to often just a few workers. For instance, when I went to Baltimore in 1969 there was very large steel works employing over 30,000 people. By the time you get to the 1990s, they are producing the same amount of steel but only 5,000 people or so are employed. By the time you get into the 2000s the steel works is either closed down or it gets re-opened after acquisition with a thousand workers. The steel workers' union was a very powerful institution in the city when I first knew it in 1969. But now, of course, it's mainly dealing with retired people and pensioners. The union has very little presence in Baltimore city politics anymore.

It is tempting to say the working class has disappeared. But when you think about it maybe it hasn't disappeared. It is simply not making the same things anymore and it's not caught up in the same activities. For example, why would we say that making automobiles or making steel is a working-class occupation, whereas making hamburgers is not? If you look at the employment data there has been a massive increase in McDonald's, and Kentucky Fried Chicken, Burger King, and all the rest. There has been a massive increase in employment in those areas. These workers are producing value just like autoworkers. It's just that they are producing prepared foods, rather than steel and automobiles. This is how we should think about the "new" working class. In recent times, we have seen the fast-food workers beginning to organize and to take militant action. But given the nature of their work they are harder to organize.

What Marx would call a "class-in-itself" has been forming around the spread and growth of these new employment categories. It's now beginning to become a "class-for-itself," as it starts to struggle against McDonald's and to demand a decent minimum wage of $15 an hour, or a living wage of more than that. There is a lot of agitation going on in the fast-food production sector. But we must also consider all the small restaurant owners and their employees in a similar way. New York City has often been thought of as a parasitical city that lives off the value production created in large industrial cities elsewhere. But it is actually a city where a great deal of value is created. If you take forms of employment such as restaurant workers, there has been an enormous increase in the numbers and this corresponds to an increase in total value output. Industries of this sort are very labor-intensive. They may eventually be vulnerable to artificial intelligence, but it's still at this point in time a very significant center of employment. Whereas 40 years ago the big sources of employment were the big automobile industries and the steel industry so that it was General Motors, Ford, and so on that mattered, now the biggest employers of labor are the Kentucky Fried Chicken and the McDonald's franchises. This is one of the key places where the new working classes are to be found. But these workers are hard to organize, a lot of the labor is temporary, people work there for a while and then leave. But we see now some possibilities of organization particularly using social media, so there are some political possibilities here.

Another thing occurred to me the other day which I thought posed possibilities. I was looking out of the window of the airplane as I was leaving Dallas airport and I see this workforce. I suddenly think about all of those people who are working at the airport. In Marx's theory, transportation is value-producing. So everybody who is involved in the transport industry and in moving people and commodities from one part of the world to another is, in fact, part of a productive working class. But when you look at the kind of labor that's involved, there are all those people who are helping push the plane out, there are all those people who are helping getting the baggage on or off the plane, there are all the people inside of the airport organizing us to get on or off the planes. There are those who are servicing and cleaning the planes.

When you look at the structure of the workforce there, it is not well paid and yet it has a very singular power. What struck me also – and I have thought about this at every airport I have been to ever since – is when you take a good hard look at who it is that is doing most of the work that makes airports actually function then in the United States there is a large number of people of color, African Americans in particular, who are involved, Latinxs, some recent white immigrants from Eastern Europe and Russia, and working women. It suddenly occurred to me that actually here you have an interesting way in which to think of the composition of the contemporary working class. This class is dominated by waged women, waged African Americans and other people of color, and waged immigrants particularly Latinas and Latinos. In this configuration the mutual interests of race, gender, and class are fused at one level while the identities remain distinct throughout.

How well is this population paid and under what conditions of social security do they live? They are all pretty badly paid at the same time as they are not at all well organized. So I have this fantasy. Let's suppose all of the workers at the airport suddenly decided to withdraw their labor on a particular day such that the airport closes down. Let's suppose, six airports in the United States – Los Angeles, Chicago, Atlanta, New York, Miami, and Dallas-Fort Worth – all closed down until the demands of all such workers were met. Pretty soon, the whole country would be dysfunctional. Trump decided that it was a good idea to shut down the government for a month in January 2019. But there then came a particular day – I think it was on a Wednesday – when it turned out that three airports in the United States could not function. They had to cancel a lot of flights out of LaGuardia and a couple more airports, because the air traffic controllers (state employees) could not keep going anymore. They had been without pay for months and they just could not sustain themselves and so quite a few did not turn up to work. Interestingly, beating the air traffic controllers was one of the big anti-union moves that Reagan made back in 1982. Suddenly, it must have appeared to Trump and the administration and everyone else that within three or four days most of the airports in the United States would close down. If you close down the airports in the United States, basically you shut off capital flow. The airport workers have immense potential political power. If the airport workers were organized, you not only would actually then be dealing with relations between African Americans, Latinx, and women, which now constitutes the core of the US labor movement, but you would be actually looking at an organization of labor which had the potentiality to do serious damage to a capitalist economy unless its demands were met. Then the question arises: what would the demands of such a coalition be? Obviously, to increase wages to the point where people have a decent life, and a decent living environment. I think an all airport workers' movement would make a really big difference in terms of concretely building working-class political power.

Just think of the few times when we have become close to something of this kind happening. After 9/11, people stopped flying; for about three days, everything was quiet. Then I remember Rudolph Giuliani (then mayor of the city) and even President Bush coming on the airwaves and saying "please get out and start shopping again, please get out and start flying again." They realized that if the country did not actually get back into motion again, there would be serious losses of capital. While the immediate response to 9/11 was to shut down, immediately afterwards what we find is this urgent push to get us back into work and movement.

Then there was the Icelandic volcano which put so much ash in the air that transatlantic flights could not go through for about ten days. It was almost impossible to get from New York to London during that time, except by going down to Rio de Janeiro and then flying over to Madrid – you had to do something like that to get there. Instead of a volcano, I imagine a volcanic eruption of the airport workers. But for that to happen the airport workers have to realize (a) that they have a lot of common interests and that they have common demands that they would wish to try to articulate and to win, and (b) that they would have a commonality amongst themselves to prosecute those demands, and they have also built a commonality of power, a tremendous power to close the system down. This was the sort of thing that was in the past threatened by and sometimes done by the miners, the auto workers, and the like. But now the power to do that is located elsewhere. And it is just as potent.

The constitution of the workforce has changed. It would be good if there could be an organization bringing together all restaurant workers, not only fast-food workers, though the fast-food workforce is a good place to start. When we start to think about the contemporary working class, it's no longer the auto workers who are in the lead, it's no longer the miners who are in the lead. The heart of traditional working-class politics in Britain used to be the Miners' Union. It was essentially destroyed by a whole series of moves by Margaret Thatcher (who hated the mine workers anyway), but coal mining in Britain has essentially closed down and traditional working-class politics has almost disappeared.

In the face of this history, we have to be prepared to think about completely new configurations of the workforce that have the power to wage struggle at the point of their production activity. This struggle at the point of production is not disconnected, however, from the sorts of lifestyles which we're now living. So what goes on at the point of realization if of equal significance. In the airport workers' case, we're talking about the fact that more and more people are now using airlines, the airline industry is expanding at a very fast rate. Not so much in the United States of course, but in China, for example, they're making airports all over the place, and the flying public in China is getting larger, so that you're seeing a large increase in Asiatic air travel. This too is predicated on the development of a certain way of life, in which we can imagine that we can move freely as long as we have the money to fly across the Atlantic, or fly here, fly there, fly everywhere. The tourist industry, with its packaged flights and accommodations, is one of the fastest growing sectors of the global economy. This is again a way of life. This way of life, of course, also has some consequences and one of them which we should be really concerned about is global warming and greenhouse gas emission. One flight across the continent of the United States is equivalent to gas emissions of I don't know how many thousand cars over the whole year. This is a major source of greenhouse gases. Now, do we want to continue that kind of lifestyle where air traffic is central? So you see the point here is that the growth of air traffic is creating a working class in terms of facilitating the rise of this new lifestyle, but the growth of air traffic is itself caught up in what Marx calls the contradictory unity between production and realization.

Questions of realization are connected very strongly to questions of lifestyle, and the production of new wants, needs and desires. The want, need, and desire to travel, the want, need, and desire to be in one part of the world rather than another. These are connected questions. But here too, I think that what we see is the need to think through the relationships between what's going on in the world of realization, the production of new wants, needs, desires, and lifestyles, and what's going on at the point of production. How we organize at the point of production is therefore connected with what we would want to do about certain things which are happening at the point of realization. It is astonishing to realize how much of our contemporary economy is structured around the attempt to make real the fantasy of a total romance in a bucolic setting of sea, sand, sun, and sex.

Similar issues arise in the field of social reproduction. When I was a kid in Britain in the 1940s, all meals were cooked at home, except on Fridays when I was sent to the shop (which only opened on that day) to buy fish and chips (wrapped in newspaper which we had to supply ourselves). Otherwise, all food preparation was at home. Now we have a situation in many parts of the world in which much food preparation is commoditized and marketized. Most food preparation does not occur at home. Families have a choice: take-out from the local restaurant – using organizations like Grubhub, allowing people to buy in food prepared elsewhere. This practice is spreading quickly. I was surprised to see the last time I was in China massive numbers of bicycles with people delivering food, Chinese take-out. In China! This is the standard process whereby food preparation is being marketized and commodified. This may or may not be a good thing, we can debate its rights and wrongs. But what is I think most significant is the lifestyle that we're talking about. The production and the development of these very large take-out organizations, piled on top of the fast-food industries, such as the Burger Kings and the McDonald's and all the rest of it, has had a huge impact on everyone's daily life in the United States. When you start to put this picture together, we have to acknowledge how the qualities of a lifestyle, the how and why of certain forms of provision occurring within this lifestyle, are radically reconfiguring processes of social reproduction. It used to be that women did most of the food preparation in the home. Now, if food preparation is not occurring in the home, this has actually dealt a blow to that gender discrimination where women were essentially stuck in the kitchen doing all of the kitchen labor. Kitchen labor has been much reduced by the fact that people dine in fast-food restaurants or order in their daily food. This liberation of women's labor in social reproduction enables the absorption of more and more women into the labor force (e.g. at airports ...). This does not mean that household tasks disappear or that gender discrimination around those tasks does not persist. But the orchestration of social reproduction in relation to the politics of realization and divisions of labor has been revolutionized over the last generation.

In all of these respects, when we ask the political question "What is to be done?" we have to actually ask ourselves, what is to be done very specifically about the rise of these new lifestyles; the emergence of a certain powerful form of labor organization around say, fast food and around airports, and in the fields of logistics; and how the power of that new labor force can be mobilized in a certain kind of way for political ends. We must envision a transformation of the social order such as it moves away from being all about capital accumulation and capital structures, to something which is much more social, and much more cooperative, and much less involved in the rapid expansion of capital accumulation. But how that is to be done is the big question.

14

Carbon Dioxide Emissions and Climate Change

There are times and moments in my life when I learn something that changes everything and makes me rethink a lot of positions that I've held. Sometimes it's something I've learned theoretically. This is the sort of thing that's often come to me from closer contemplation of what Marx has to say. But on other occasions it's just a piece of information. So I came across a piece of information about four months ago that literally blew my mind and made me rethink a lot of my positions. The information was contained in a graph put out by the National Oceanic and Atmospheric Administration (NOAA). The graph depicted carbon dioxide concentrations in the atmosphere over the last 800,000 years. That seems like a long period of time, but geologically it's not so long. But it is, on the other hand, long enough to capture phases of global warming, and cooling. At no point in the last 800,000 years has the carbon dioxide concentration in the atmosphere gone above 300 parts per million (ppm). It has oscillated in fact between 150 ppm and 300 ppm over those 800,000 years, the highest points being at 300 ppm. But it hit 300 ppm sometime after 1960. Then over the last 60 years, it has gone from 300 ppm to above 400 ppm. Now that's a huge and very rapid increase. This is something way beyond anything that's been experienced over the last 800,000 years.

The implications and why it happened have been absorbing me a lot. One of the implications is that if Donald Trump learns about it he will abolish the NOAA, the organization that published this document, or at least instruct it that it shall not put out any more information of this kind. But the increase and the incredible amount of it means that the amount of carbon dioxide in the atmosphere is already very high and something which is almost certainly inimical to the continuation of human habitation in the way we know it. All the ice on Earth doesn't just melt overnight, it's going to take 50, maybe 100 years to do it, but it's going to go, full stop. And if it goes, we're going to get rapid sea rise (the Greenland ice cap is already diminishing), the Himalaya snowpack is going to disappear, which means the Indus and the Ganges rivers are essentially going to run dry at certain times of the year. There will be chronic drought through all of the Indian sub-continent and the rest of the world will suffer immense transformations.

Where did this 400 ppm come from, and what happened? I am here going to venture on to some awkward terrain because one answer is what has happened in China. I will get to that in a minute. But we must first acknowledge something else about the dynamics of climate change, which is that its runaway character means that if climate change melts the Arctic permafrost (which it is already doing), then the melting of the permafrost will release methane gases (a far more virulent greenhouse gas than carbon dioxide) so as to produce even more rapid climate change.

The NOAA data changed my attitude to the question of climate change and what to do about it. Here, I have to backtrack a little bit to talk about the general view I have taken about environmental questions and environmental issues over the last 60 years since I first became conscious of environmental questions. When I was a student there was a great deal of agitation in the world around the idea that the Earth was running out of a viable and sustaining resource base. The resource that people were worried about the most at the time was energy – oil and fossil fuel possibilities in particular. This was in the 1950s into the 1960s. Throughout the 1960s there was further agitation, and by the time you got to 1970 (the year of the first Earth Day) there was a great deal of preoccupation about the limits to growth set by the natural resource base but now including problems of pollution and the use of the Earth as a waste dump. A significant literature was coming out suggesting that the environmental capacities of the Earth were not limitless and that therefore an environmental crisis was impending.

The first Earth Day marked a time when even corporate America started to wake up to the fact that there might be an environmental problem. *Forbes* magazine had a special issue on the limits that existed in the environment. The first essay in that magazine special issue was by President Richard Nixon and basically said that we have to care about the environment, we can't always dominate it. There was an acceptance on the part of political power that there might be some issue here. *Forbes* magazine had some wonderful ideas about what should happen and in particular on urbanization, there were designs for new cities, and the designs for new cities that had a lot of trees around – there was plenty of evidence for what we now call "greenwashing" on the part of the corporate sector.

But there was a more radical wing of the movement that blamed capitalism for the ills. Faced with the oil spill off the coast of Santa Barbara, California, students at the university there buried a Chevy in the sands as a sort of symbolic protest against the excessive use of and reliance on fossil fuels. There was a great deal of agitation at the time going to the first Earth Day in 1970. Many people were disturbed about the qualities of the food chain, air qualities, and the like. But what struck me at an Earth Day event in the city of Baltimore was that in a city where half the population was African American, there were hardly any African Americans present. It was entirely a white middle-class audience in attendance. The same week I went to this Earth Day event, I went to the Left Bank jazz club in Baltimore, which was a predominantly black institution, with just a smattering of white people around. The music was great. The musicians on that occasion talked about environmental problems to great cheers from the audience. Their version was "our biggest environmental problem is Richard Nixon." Plainly, there is a huge gap in framing what constitutes an environmental problem.

This experience made me very nervous about a lot of the environmentalist rhetoric. In particular, I resisted that wing of the environmentalist movement that proclaimed that apocalypse is nigh, that the world is going to run out of resources, that everything is going to collapse into environmental disaster. I've always resisted such apocalyptic renditions, which is not to say that I thought environmental questions were irrelevant or not, in certain dimensions, serious. In fact, I think they are very relevant and I think we need to deal with them as they come up. It is just that I didn't share a lot of the apocalyptic visions which were around at that time and which have been around ever since. Without the apocalyptic vision, the approach to environmental questions is one of taking them seriously and managing them so that we deal with air, water pollution, and carbon concentrations through regulation, regulatory activity, and the like, and we don't get into a panic that it has to be done tomorrow or everything is going to collapse.

Back in the 1970s there was this famous bet between Julian Simon, an economist, and Paul Ehrlich, an environmentalist who insisted that the world was overpopulated and that we were going to run out of resources and that the food supply was going to be curtailed, and that we were courting disaster. Julian Simon denied this was the case. So they made a bet in which Julian Simon said that in ten years' time, we're going to see that all basic commodity prices are going to be lower than they were then, which signals that there's not a serious problem of inherent scarcities in the environment. Ehrlich took the bet and ten years later they looked at all the commodity prices and Julian Simon won the bet.

Since then some people have pointed out Ehrlich lost the wager because 1970 was a bad year to start the bet. In other words, if you start the bet at a time when commodity prices are particularly high, the likelihood is strong that they're going to go down over the following decade. If you started it when commodity prices were low, it would be the other way around. As somebody has pointed out since, if you started the bet in 1980 and looked at what happened to the prices between 1980 and 1990, Ehrlich would have been right. So this question of "are we in a difficult environmental situation or are we not?" has been around for a long time. There are cornucopians, those who think there is an almost limitless capacity of the environment to absorb what human beings are doing, and the apocalyptic scenario folk, who think there is going to be an environmental crash. There is the Malthusian bet made 200 years ago that said that compounding rates of global population growth will inevitably encounter constraints of natural resources to produce international famine and poverty and along with social degradation, violence and war.

There's been a long-standing debate about all of this. I've always taken the view that we should take environmental questions seriously but I have been profoundly skeptical of apocalyptic scenarios and visions. But that really changed when I saw that 400 ppm of carbon dioxide concentrations against the background that nothing above 300 ppm had been seen for the last 800,000 years. This 400+ figure says it's not the *rate* of carbon emissions that we should be looking at and controlling, but we have to start to look at the *absolute level* of greenhouse gas concentrations already in the atmosphere. The current level guarantees accelerating desiccation, rapid increase in global temperatures, rapidly rising sea levels, an increasing frequency of extreme weather patterns, and the like. This suggests that the policy of restricting the rate of carbon emissions, which is what we mainly talk about these days, has to be changed.

There is an urgent problem to decrease the existing concentrations of greenhouse gases (carbon dioxide and methane). In Chapter 9 I talked about the difference between thinking about the world in terms of the rates of change and thinking about the world in terms of absolute masses of change. And I mentioned the case in which if you have a very low initial level, you can have a very high rate of change with very little impact. If you have a very high mass, then a small rate of change can produce a vast increase in the mass.

But where did the recent increase in mass of carbon dioxide in the atmosphere come from. The data shows that one of the sources came with the development in China after 2000. This development entailed a massive development in infrastructures. I have been fond of showing a graph of cement utilization in China. This increased hugely such that China consumed in two and a half years about 45 percent more cement than the United States consumed in 100 years. China had been expanding at a very rapid rate from the 1990s onwards, but this process accelerated enormously in the crisis of 2007–08, because China's export market (to the United States) collapsed and it therefore substituted an infrastructural program of development that would have been unthinkable anywhere else in the world. While the rest of the world went into austerity, China went into expansionism.

I earlier argued that China saved global capitalism from a crash in 2007–08 by undertaking this massive infrastructural expansion. It didn't do this because it wanted to but because this was the only way in which it could absorb its surplus labor problem produced by the crash of the export industries. So China saved global capitalism at the expense of a massive increase in greenhouse gas emissions. This is in part where the leap to more than 400 ppm comes from. But China was not the only place that was developing in this way. If you look at expansionism in Brazil and Turkey during these years, you'll find some of the same sorts of things going on in response to the crash of 2007–08 with commensurable impacts upon greenhouse gas emissions.

The first implication is that we cannot confine discussion to limiting rates of change but recognize the importance of the existing mass. We need to consider how to extract carbon dioxide out of the atmosphere as much as we can. That is partly done naturally through the absorption of carbon dioxide into oceans where it gets turned by shellfish into shells, and so on. This is a natural way of absorption. But we need to come up with ways of carbon absorption through agriculture. It is the release of the carbon concentrations underground, of the energy stored eons ago in preceding epochs, that lies at the root of our contemporary problems. The carbon we are taking out from underground needs to be put back underground if we are to return to a world of 300 ppm. It was originally put underground by vegetation, and to some degree crustaceans. We've taken all of that stored energy from underground and now released it. We now need to talk seriously about getting that 400 back down to 300 ppm and the only way we can do that is by finding means of getting the carbon dioxide out of the atmosphere and back underground.

One of the ways we can do this is through reforestation. But reforestation is limited to new growth forests. Reforesting the world would reduce the carbon dioxide content of the atmosphere. There have been reforestation schemes, and in the Northern hemisphere there has been a net increase of forest cover. The big problem areas are the tropical rain forests in the Amazon, in Sumatra, Borneo, and in Africa, which have all experienced an incredible attack. The deforestation of Amazonia and in Southeast Asia is tragically continuing to accelerate. Bolsonaro coming to power in Brazil is the same as Donald Trump, he doesn't believe in any of this climate change nonsense, and so they're actually going to expand the attack upon Amazonia in order to open it up to soybean cultivation, beef raising, and all the rest of it. So, the struggle over protecting the tropical rain forest and reforestation is one critical arena for political action.

Another option – and I am not an expert on this, and I've only come across this recently so some of you may want to go out there and check this out – is there are forms of cultivation which take the carbon dioxide and put it back underground. Now, you can put it underground 6 inches but if you deep plow then you release it again. There's going to have to be a radical change in agricultural technology and agricultural techniques. But there are also crops which put the carbon dioxide 6 feet underground, they take it deep down underground, which means there is a deep-rooted system that takes the carbon dioxide and puts it in that depth. If we can cultivate crops of that kind, then we could start a process of extracting the carbon dioxide from the atmosphere and putting it back in the ground.

This is a very important possibility. But how do we get farmers to do this? And what will it take, what impact will it have on agriculture? There is one sign of hope here. In the European Union and also in the United States, there are programs which pay farmers not to grow anything because there is an agricultural surplus. This means taking some land out of production. Well, instead of paying farmers to grow nothing, why wouldn't we pay them to grow the kinds of crops which actually put the carbon dioxide back in the ground? But how much of this would we have to do in order to get concentrations down from 400 to 300 ppm? I have no idea, but these are the sorts of techniques and technologies that need to be deployed. So, in terms of the production of greenhouse gas emissions, we need to seriously consider how to take carbon dioxide out of the atmosphere and put it back underground from whence it came. The only other futuristic way is to design and build huge carbon extraction machines that will bury the carbon underground.

It was in this way that the graph of carbon dioxide concentrations over the last 800,000 years changed everything in my world view. The question of climate change went from something I thought to be manageable by normal techniques and sensible interventions to a recognition of the need for a radical transformation of all of our ways of thinking, all of our ways of doing and living, not only in terms of reducing our fossil fuel consumption and reducing the rate of carbon emissions, but also starting now to think more seriously about finding ways to bring the carbon dioxide out of the atmosphere and put it back where it came from, which is underground.

We need to think more seriously about the climate change problem and carbon dioxide emissions – and to think about ways to control and curb the continuing increase of those emissions, particularly in China and in all emerging markets around the world. But as those countries complain when governments from the United States, or Britain, or Europe say that "you shouldn't be doing this," they respond correctly that "you did it for 100 years and you got to be developed to where you are right now, so why shouldn't we do it for the next 100 years?" Carbon emissions from India, from China, and from Brazil and Turkey have all been increasing. We need to find a way to construct economic development which is not based on increasing carbon intensity and the increasing use of fossil fuels.

There is an emergency here that needs to be addressed in our thinking and in our economic and political practices. But notice that in all of this the big problem in the background is capital accumulation. It was, after all, the drive for capital accumulation in China that required that they develop in the way they did. If global capitalism after 2007–08 was largely rescued by China and by the emerging markets who engaged in this radical expansion that produced a surge in greenhouse gas emissions, then we have a situation in which the survival of capitalism depended upon an expansionist project in all those countries at the expense of rapidly rising carbon dioxide emissions. But it is the existing concentrations, I now insist, that are the problem. The global community has to address this – as quickly as possible – and this cannot happen without calling into question the driving force behind it all which is that of endless and compounding rates of capital accumulation.

15

Rate versus Mass of Surplus Value

When I teach Marx's *Capital* Volume I, the first chapter introduces us to the idea of value. Value, according to Marx, is socially necessary labor time. Invariably, a student will then pop up and say: "What happens when there is a firm that doesn't employ any labor, does that mean that they produce no value?" This question has become more and more significant in recent years, given the looming idea of artificial intelligence taking over a lot of the activities of human labor. It's a perfectly reasonable question, but it has an intriguing answer, which I want to spend a little time thinking about.

In a later chapter of Volume I of *Capital*, Marx examines the relationship between the rate and mass of surplus value. He asks: are capitalists more interested in the mass of surplus value or the rate at which they gain it? Many people familiar with Marx tend to think that capitalists focus most on the rate since they know Marx emphasizes the falling rate of profit in Volume III. But in the first volume of *Capital* it is the mass that is the main focus, because it's the mass that gives capitalists their power. Increasing the rate is simply seen as one means to increase the mass.

Marx unfurls another contradiction in that chapter. Let me read it to you, because he's very alert, I think, to the way in which socially necessary labor time is dependent upon the nature of the technology and the nature of the labor process. He notes towards the end of this chapter how the masses of value and surplus value produced by different capitals vary according to the labor they employ. This signals a contradiction. Everyone knows, he writes, "that a cotton spinner, who employs a great deal of capital and very little labor, does not on account of this pocket less profit or surplus value than a baker, who sets in motion relatively much labor power and very little means of production. For the solution of this apparent contradiction," says Marx, "many intermediate terms are still needed." Now, when Marx says something like that, you know that somewhere else in his vast amount of work, you're going to find a solution to this particular contradiction. If not a solution to it, an elaboration of it, which will explain how the contradiction works.

We also know that when Marx is writing Volume I of *Capital*, he's already produced the notes which became the basis of the Volume III of *Capital*. So we immediately go to Volume III to see what he says about this. The answer is given in the chapter on the equalization of the rate of profit. Capitalists, when they are working in the market, are interested in the profit rate, not the rate of surplus value, which measures the exploitation of living labor in production. Since capitalists compete with each other over the profit rate, the tendency in the long run will be to converge and to produce a standard profit rate for all companies, all firms, no matter whether they're employing a lot of labor or not.

If this is the case, then what in effect happens is a transfer of value from those companies, and firms, and regions, which are engaging in labor-intensive activities to those regions, firms, and sections of society which are engaging in capital-intensive modes of production. In other words, there is a transfer of value from labor-intensive to capital-intensive forms of production. This is sometimes referred to as a form of "capitalist communism." The rule is this: "from each capitalist according to the labor they employ, and to each capitalist according to the capital they advance." A subsidy flows from labor-intensive forms of production, and labor-intensive economies, to firms and economies which are capital-intensive. This transfer of value occurs through competition over the rate of profit in the market. It is an effect of perfectly competitive markets and it is one of Marx's most significant findings.

This raises interesting questions: for instance, if you are a decision-maker and you have to decide which kind of industrialization you want, do you want labor-intensive or do you want capital-intensive? The answer is, if you go for labor-intensive forms you're going to transfer value to the capital-intensive forms. A sensible decision-maker would say: I don't want to industrialize with labor-intensive industry. One economy that I think is a very good example of this is Singapore. Singapore, when it was thrown out of the Malaysian Federation in the early 1960s, had to figure out what it was going to do and what kind of industrial strategy it was going to have. What Singapore decided was that they were not going to go to labor-intensive activities of the sort that were in Hong Kong and elsewhere, they were going to go for capital-intensive. That's what they did. Singapore is a very good example of the advantages that are attached to engaging in capital-intensive forms of production. This explains why so many economies which enter the world market through labor-intensive industrialization either stay poor (like Bangladesh) or seek to transform to capital-intensive economic forms (as did Japan, South Korea, Taiwan and now China).

This transfer and consequent subsidy is something which needs study. Through the equalization of the rate of profit, we get a transfer of value from the labor-intensive economies and firms to the capital-intensive economies and firms. This transfer is sustained and it therefore helps explain why it is that low-productivity economies, when they get inserted into a situation where they're competing with highly productive economies, end up subsidizing the more capital-intensive economies. For example, when Greece entered the European Union, Greece had a labor-intensive, low productivity economy in relationship to Germany, which has a capital-intensive economy. The result is that Greece subsidizes Germany. This will come as a huge shock to the Germans because the popular German view is that the money they're lending to the impoverished Greeks is because the Greeks are lazy and idle and culturally backward. No, the problem for Greece is that they have a low productivity labor regime. And that means that no matter how hard they work, most of the value they create is going to be siphoned off to Germany by free market mechanisms that tend to equalize the rate of profit. Free trade is not fair trade at all.

This is the way this economy works and right now, we're beginning to see something that is very important, which is a fight over capital intensity and which economies are allowed to be capital-intensive.

I'll get back to the mechanisms of this in a short while, but the basic thing here is that China has long relied upon a labor-intensive economy but has recently announced that it's going to move towards a more capital-intensive economy. If it does that, then the transfer of value that occurs from China to the capital-intensive economies of Europe and the United States is going to diminish. There is a battle going on between Trump and the Chinese over intellectual property rights and over technology. Now technology is, of course, the handmaid of capital intensity. The United States is trying to prevent the transfer of technological know-how to China, so that China is to be kept in a state of a labor-intensive economy for the benefit of the United States. But China cannot sustain labor intensity anymore, partly for demographic reasons – they're running into shortages of labor – and partly for other reasons that have to do with the nature of the market.

Labor-intensive forms of production are being moved out of China and into Cambodia, Laos, Vietnam, and even Bangladesh. Here I think it's useful to look at the trajectory of, say, Singapore, which chose a capital-intensive path, and Bangladesh, which has a labor-intensive path. You see immediately that Bangladesh is a very troubled economy and is not doing very well at all, even though it is producing a great deal of value because of all of the labor it employs. On the other hand, Singapore is acquiring a great deal of value even though it's not employing that much labor. There's a transfer going on from Bangladesh and economies like Bangladesh to Singapore. Part of the tense relation that now exists between the United States and China is over capital transfer. The Chinese goal is to shift to a capital-intensive economy by 2025, which of course would be a rival to the United States. Trump seems hell-bent on stopping them.

The importance of this issue is generally acknowledged within Marxist circles. But Michael Roberts has recently complained on his website that the transfer of value from the poor capitalist economies with lower levels of technology to the rich imperialist economies has been greatly neglected by Marxist economists in recent times. What is it then that we're going to see through this transfer of value from labor-intensive to capital-intensive sectors and economies? The main thing is a tendency for those areas which are capital intense to draw to themselves much greater capital intensity. This is something that was laid out early on by Swedish economist Gunnar Myrdal. He pointed to mechanisms that exist by means of which rich regions get richer while poor regions either stagnate or decline, under conditions of free trade and profit equalization. This process Myrdal called "circular and cumulative causation." It occurs because capital is inevitably attracted to the dynamic sectors, cities, and regions, draining the less dynamic sectors, cities, and regions of their wealth, population, resources, talents, and skills.

Marx had even earlier noticed this dynamic. Here I quote from him in *Capital*: "ease of commerce and the consequent acceleration in the turnover of capital gives rise to an accelerated concentration of both the center of production and its market. With this accelerated concentration of people and capital at given points, the concentration of these masses of capital in a few hands makes rapid progress." What we're dealing with in capitalist economies is a sucking sound, echoing how value is being extracted from the whole of the world, and being agglomerated in areas of great capital intensity and technological advantage. There is a strong tendency – and this is something which I think is being remarked upon about the capitalist economy in these times – for the large metropolitan centers (like New York, Chicago, and San Francisco) to draw in all of the talent, all of the capital, and thereby become the centers of capitalist dynamics and capitalist growth, and also the centers where great personal fortunes are going to be made. If you look at the United States, for example, you will find that about two-thirds of the GDP is created in about a dozen of the largest metropolitan centers. The metropoles have become irresistible magnets for both capital and for talent.

Now, this is an interesting process because the classical, and later the neoclassical, economists anchored their arguments on the supposed neutrality and inherent equality and fairness of perfectly functioning markets. But what you're now seeing is how perfectly functioning markets turn out to be unfair markets when the profit rate gets equalized. In other words, the assumption that a market system can be fair is destroyed through the equalization of the rate of profit. We can go even further and say that perhaps the most unfair way in which a capitalist system can be organized is to have a market system through which the equalization of the profit rate occurs, because it appears as if it is egalitarian and fair when it is not. This is a classic case of how "there is nothing more unequal than the equal treatment of unequals." The equalization of the rate of profit produces the uneven geographical development of wealth and power.

So when do we have the equalization of the rate of profit? This has to be looked at historically. Marx, in effect, says the equalization of the rate of profit creates unfair structures of trade in which the rich regions grow richer and the poor regions grow poorer, and the rich states grow richer and the poor states grow poorer. The neoclassical economists' argument is that free market is fair trade and that therefore they're going to produce egalitarian outcomes, whereas Marx's argument is no, you're going to produce highly concentrated forms of wealth and privilege. So one sign that the equalization of the rate of profit is occurring will be increasing regional, national, and social inequality.

When Marx was writing, there was not really a very good system for equalizing the profit rate because for many commodities the transport costs were very high and there were a lot of tariffs and barriers to trade. In the 1860s, the capacity to equalize the profit rate was not that strong even locally and certainly not internationally. But it began to be stronger because of innovations in communications and transport – the coming of the railroads and the steamships and the telegraph meant that there could be at least equalization of prices on major commodities across the world. Traders in London would have information about the wheat prices in Buenos Aires, Odessa, and Chicago, so there was a closer approximation to equalizing the rate of profit through transport and communications. But what we see later on is this construction of a global trading system where the equalization of the rate of profit was not a priority. The Bretton-Woods agreement, for example, was an agreement in which capital could not easily move around the world because of capital controls. The US economy was not a closed economy, but was relatively closed because it was hard to move capital in and out of the United States.

At that time the US economy could reasonably be looked upon as if it was an economy in its own right. There would be workers struggling within that economy for advantages, and the labor movement would be working within it. The organization of production within that economy could even have a monopolistic character, so that, for example, if you read the classic texts on monopoly capitalism by Paul Sweezy and Paul A. Baran, what they would say is that Detroit was a very good example of what monopoly capitalism is about. In this case, just three major firms which did price leadership and were involved with each other. But as far as Sweezy and Baran were concerned, that was the kind of typical example you would use when you wanted to talk about monopolistic structures. There was no competition in the 1960s from, say, German and Japanese firms, they came in much later in the 1970s and 1980s.

Labor struggled for advantage within the United States, as it did within Britain, as it did within France, as it did within Germany. We could talk about a German working class, a French working class, a British working class, and an American working class. Each one of those working classes could seek advantage within a defined terrain, because they were largely protected from having to compete with labor in all the other economies in the world because of the system of capital controls. This system of capital controls lasted up until the breakdown of the Bretton-Woods system, which occurred when the dollar went off the gold standard in 1971. After that, labor suddenly found itself having to compete with all of the labor forces elsewhere in the world. Before that, its only competition came through the organization of immigration from elsewhere. Germany imported Turkish labor, France imported labor from North Africa, the Maghrebian labor, the Swedes imported labor from Yugoslavia and Portugal, the British imported labor from its once upon a time imperial area, from South Asia, and from the West Indies, and the United States opened up its immigration system in 1965.

During the 1960s, the main problem for labor came from the way in which immigration was being deployed to try to undermine both the labor laws and the labor capacities. What that led to, then, was the rise of a certain anti-immigrant sentiment within many of the working-class movements across Europe and even to some degree in the United States. We're seeing that of course very much revived right now. However, in the 1970s, suddenly, capital controls were abolished, and capital could start to move freely from one part of the world to another. The abolition of capital control barriers was supplemented by reductions in transport costs and improved communications to make capital highly mobile. Finally, after the 1980s in particular, we start to see the emergence of a situation where the equalization of the profit rate becomes more and more significant.

So what I'm suggesting here is that the historical conditions under which the equalization of the profit rate was going to be set up were lacking throughout much of the nineteenth century, and until the end of the Bretton-Woods period. But what has really marked what the period of globalization has been about since the 1980s onwards has been that equalization of the profit rate could occur, which means that during this period we're likely to see much more transfer of value going on from labor-intensive economies to capital-intensive economies. In other words, the distinction between labor-intensive and capital-intensive economies has moved to the fore. It's therefore become now a focus of struggle, a fierce struggle to try to prevent certain areas of the world becoming capital-intensive. This is what the United States is trying to do in relationship to China right now.

Why is the United States so upset at the fact that China wants to become a capital-intensive economy by 2025? Why are they so upset with the technology transfers which have occurred to China? And why therefore is there this big struggle over intellectual property rights, which is the main thing which is creating the problems right now in negotiations between Trump and the Chinese? So we have then a situation where, historically, the contrast between labor-intensive and capital-intensive economies was not so significant, even though Marx saw it as theoretically significant and theoretically important when he was writing *Capital* in the middle of the nineteenth century. But we've now got to the point where what Marx saw as being a possible feature of a capitalist economy in a pure state has now actually arrived. This is, therefore, why we're seeing this emergent conflict between the United States and China over technology.

16

Alienation

Alienation is a concept that has a somewhat checkered history on the left. But there is a very good reason why today we might want to revive it. I think it has great relevance to helping us understand the relationships between politics and the economy. Part of the reason for the checkered history is that Marx in his early years was fond of talking about alienation and it played a prominent role in his thinking when he wrote the *Economic and Philosophic Manuscripts of 1844*. But at that time the definition of alienation that Marx held was based on the idea that our daily reality was not in accord with our species potentiality. Marx in those years had a rather idealist notion of humanity. This idealism underpinned his concept of species being. His argument was that capital was preventing us from realizing the perfection of which we were capable given our species being. It was an idealist concept, a utopian concept, but it played a very important role in defining the subjective feelings of alienation, loss, and separation that arose within the working class in relationship to the domination of capital.

Alienation was not entirely redundant as a scientific concept, but its basis lay in this rather humanist conception of what human beings are capable of, and the frustrations of that capacity by being embedded within a market system in which the capitalist class held the power. This ideal of alienation in the early writings was problematic even for Marx himself. By the time he got to the end of the 1840s he was proposing a different interpretation in which he did not rely upon the idealist conception of species being. He relied more and more on historical interrogation of the concepts, which would reflect the relationships actually existing under capitalism. Marx sought a more scientific approach in which alienation as an idealist concept did not fit. For that reason, there arose a tendency within the history of Marxism, very strong in the 1960s and 1970s, to erase alienation from the scientific forms of Marxism favored by people like Althusser, theoretically, and by the communist parties which existed in Europe at that time, politically. This erasure closely followed the communist doctrines then promoted in the Soviet Union.

From the 1960s on, the concept of alienation was generally abandoned within Marxism (with the exception of the Marxist humanists such as Erich Fromm) on the grounds that it was un-scientific and un-verifiable. It was not considered to be a part of what socialist and communist science should be about. But the argument that Marx himself abandoned the concept of alienation in the late 1840s does not fit very well with the fact that in 1857–58 he wrote the *Grundrisse* in which the concept of alienation comes back into the picture in a big way. But it took a very different form, played a very different role, and therefore had a very different meaning from that conveyed in the 1844 manuscripts.

In the *Grundrisse*, it looks like this: if we become separated from something which belongs to us, and we lose control over it, we become alienated from it. Marx argued that the very act of exchange from one person to another meant that there is an alienation of a commodity as it is traded away. Alienation has a technical meaning. But then that meant that as you built an understanding of how the market system works, that technical meaning took on broader significance.

In the *Grundrisse*, Marx examines how the laborer is alienated from the labor process, alienated in the following sense: that they are employed by capital, they produce a commodity, but they do not actually have any power over the commodity they have produced, nor do they have any right to the value which is embodied in that commodity. The labor power which the laborer provides is alienated from its product. But this is a technical alienation which rests on the fact that the value created by the laborer belongs to capital and the commodity belongs to capital. Furthermore, command over the labor process itself moves away from the laborer. The laborer who commands tools and skills still has a certain power in defining how things are produced, but as time goes on and machinery is introduced and the factory system comes into being, then the laborer becomes an appendage of the machine, alienated from the labor process as well as from the product. The labor process, the labor product, and the value therein, all of them are alienated from the laborer. That loss underpins a political claim, which says that we should invent the kind of society in which laborers can reclaim rights over the value and the commodity that they have produced.

But it's not only the laborer who is alienated. Marx argues that the capitalist experiences a similar problem. The capitalist, in bourgeois theory at least, is a free juridical individual endowed with private property rights trading in an egalitarian market system. The starting point for capital accumulation is one in which the capitalist is "free to choose," as Milton Friedman would put it, and enjoys the freedom of choice and egalitarianism that comes from market exchange. Marx then has to address how this market system, which he agrees is based on the universality of equality and freedom, gets turned into inequality and un-freedom, even for the capitalists. The answer is that individuals do not ·control the market system. In fact, that system forces capitalists into certain kinds of activities whether they like it or not. "The coercive laws of competition" rule over the behaviors of individual capitalists who are therefore not free to choose. The market disciplines them to do this or to do that. This view is common to both Marx and Adam Smith. The latter argued that the hidden hand of the market had the power to merge all kinds of entrepreneurial motivations and desires and that none of that mattered to the outcome because it was the hidden hand of the market that ruled. Adam Smith simply presumed that the outcome would be of benefit to all – a conclusion that Marx disputed and disproved decisively in *Capital*. But Marx and Smith agreed that the capitalists were also alienated from their product.

In the *Grundrisse*, Marx explains how alienated labor and alienated capital meet in the labor process. This double alienation is foundational for what the capitalist mode of production is all about. Alienation is therefore centrally embedded within the capitalist system. It returns as a key scientific concept in building a critical theory of capital. While Althusser influentially argued that Marx went through an epistemological break in 1848 when he switched from a language of alienation to one in which that concept had no place, Marx's revival of the concept in 1858 would suggest that there is a way of bringing it back into our understanding of political economy. But the 1858 version is a very different concept of alienation to that which Marx had promoted in 1844.

This comes out most clearly in Marx's chapter in *Capital* on the working day. We there see that the capitalist employs the laborer for a certain period of time as a use value that has the power to create value. The laborer gets the exchange value equivalent of the value of labor power as a commodity and the capitalist extends the working day to create a surplus value which underpins profit. Surplus value is labor appropriated by capital. This is the alienation that the laborer experiences. The coercive laws of competition force capitalists to maximize the exploitation of the labor power they employ. If I only employ my workers for six hours a day, but somebody else is competing with me and employing their labor for eight hours a day at the same wage, then I will soon be driven out of business. Very soon, all capitalists extend the working day as much as they can to outcompete all rivals. This competition between individual capitalists forces individual capitalists, no matter whether they are good people or bad people, to extend the working day to a maximum, unless there is some mechanism which is going to stop them. The mechanism is state legislation which controls the length of the working day. A ten-hour or eight-hour working day or a 40-hour working week puts a floor under the labor exploitation that arises out of the dual alienation of labor and capital in the labor process.

But we can take the question of alienation further and ask to what degree does the laborer get satisfaction out of the labor process and from the commodities that they produce? Here we come back to the subjective side of things that Marx broached in 1844. Capital is ruled by abstractions. To the degree that the ruling ideas of the ruling class hold sway, there is no room for critique. This ignores the subjectivity of workers who feel exploited and neither appreciated nor respected for the work they do. Subjective feelings of alienation come back in. Working people feel alienated by their conditions of employment, alienated by the fact that the work they put in is not adequately remunerated, that they have no command whatsoever over the production process, because it is regulated remotely from outside through the use of machinery. The time of the worker is alienated by capital because the time regime is dictated by conditions of work within the labor process. In all those respects, it can be argued that the conditions of alienation are latent within any workforce and are likely, politically, to be expressed through worker opposition and increasing class consciousness of their subjective condition. At this point the subjectivity of alienation which is described in the *Economic and Philosophic Manuscripts* comes back into the picture, but is no longer an alienation from the perfection of which we are capable, but an alienation produced by the daily grind of going to work every day and working those hours and receiving only a miniscule amount of remuneration. Not being treated with dignity and respect is the cruelest blow of all. The conditions of labor, then, are likely to give rise to powerful political feelings of alienation. The rise of rampant anti-capitalist discontents requires that we reignite and revitalize the concept of alienation in our thinking and in our politics.

Alienation has powerful subjective consequences. It is very difficult to imagine a productive labor force that deeply supports laboring if it feels alienated. The subjective condition of alienation creates a distance between the labor process and the sense of satisfaction of pride that can be derived from it. This doesn't mean that it's impossible for workers to feel any sense of satisfaction. Labor processes can be organized by workers themselves in such a way as to be interesting, with a sense of personal value attached. Workers often exhibit a sense of pride in the work that they do. You will find labor forces employed under capital where there is some degree of contentment, and there are strategies which emerge amongst the capitalists to try to encourage what's called "X-efficiency" by developing certain social relations within the workforce or between the workforce and the supervisors and the capitalists, which can compensate for the alienation. In the 1970s, for example, "quality circles" were set up in automobile manufacturing in which workers would get together and decide for themselves how they would organize their labor on the shop floor. Friendly competition between work gangs would animate the workplace. Situations arose in which workers might feel less alienated because of subjective conditions even though the underlying objective alienation remained in place.

There is for the most part, however, a profound dissatisfaction with labor process conditions under capitalism. There are surveys which suggest that about 50 percent or 70 percent of the US labor force are either not interested in their work, don't care about it, or even hate it. This is in the nature of the capitalist labor process, because the capitalist is not free to choose any more than the laborer can. Mechanized and automated labor processes proliferate so workers have no serious creative or interesting role to play. These are the most profitable labor processes that the capitalists are forced to introduce. I think it's no accident that those quality work circles that arose in the 1970s and 1980s disappeared in the 1980s as competition heated up between the different auto companies. Capital does not freely choose what its technology should be, and it does not freely choose the conditions of labor that it will impose upon a workforce when it comes through the factory gates.

Beyond that of course we also need to recognize the impacts of the emergence of new divisions of labor, along with the disappearance of many industrial jobs and the rise of rather meaningless service and guard-type jobs with no real content or physical satisfactions. As labor processes have become affected by automation and most recently by artificial intelligence, the rise of job structures which have some satisfaction attached to them appears less and less likely. In fact, we could divide roughly what goes on in society into two categories of labor: one is the more challenging mental labor, and the other is the routine manual labor in industry and the routine labor in many of the service industries like banking and so on.

We need to take a close look at contemporary conditions of labor. How much alienation is there? Is there a widespread and increasing sense of alienation with the employment structures and with the loss of regularity and increasing precarity of work? Are there diminishing satisfactions in the labor process today compared to many years ago? In what sense would we argue that the advent of a socialist economy will be an attempt to so minimize alienating labor that the alienating labor is reduced to something that is automated, artificial intelligence takes it all over and therefore we don't need people to do boring routine tasks anymore, which will free up time for everybody to be able to do what they want. One of the big signs of a socialist society is one where there is an abundance of free time for everybody, where people are emancipated from wants and needs, and find themselves able to live in that world that Marx described when he said, "the realm of freedom begins when the realm of necessity is left behind." The implication is that if we can take care of all the necessities, do all of the alienating work through automation, reduce the alienating jobs to just a few hours a week or something of that kind, then the rest of the time we can do what we want in the way that we want.

Alienation in the labor process comes back into Marx's argument in the *Grundrisse* in this way. While the word alienation does not actually crop up very much in Marx's *Capital*, the fact of alienation is all over the place. Marx is concerned with the way in which workers get turned into appendages of machines, that they move from being in control of their means of production to being controlled by the means of production. Marx also talks about the alienation that attaches to the way in which the working day is set up, he talks about alienation in terms of the decision-making of the labor process. In effect, he tacitly resurrects the categories to which he appealed in the *Economic and Philosophic Manuscripts*. He emphasizes how the laborer is not in control of the value nor of the commodity they produce which belongs to capital; they're not in control of the labor process. The alienation which exists there is important; and beyond that there is an alienated relationship to nature. The extractivism in the metabolic relation to nature is accelerating. Capital, unchecked, destroys the two primary sources of its own wealth: the laborer and the soil.

All of the forms of alienation described in the *Economic and Philosophic Manuscripts* can be found in *Capital* but they are now embedded in the scientific understanding of the accumulation of capital. Both the laborer and the capitalist are alienated, driven by abstractions and the laws of motion of capital that are fetishized and objectified by the ruling ideas of the ruling class. That is one part of the alienation story that needs to be recognized as even more important in today's world. This is the source of many current discontents.

So far I have discussed alienation in the labor process and the extension of that alienation through transformations in divisions of labor, the rise of meaningless jobs and increasing problems of alienation, stemming from tensions in the capital-labor relation and increasing extractivism from nature. From the 1960s and 1970s onwards, many workers became increasingly aware of their alienation and became actively involved in trying to do something about it. Demands arose to restructure labor processes in ways which were less alienating, to set up worker shop floor councils, to build worker cooperatives and other forms of worker associations to organize production in a very different way. Some Marxists, such as André Gorz, argued that this was a losing struggle and that something else was going on which was far more important. The uprisings of 1968 focused on demands of young people for individual liberty and freedom and social justice. The response of the capitalist class and the corporations was to try to satisfy these demands by paying closer attention to the wants, needs and desires of the younger generation by restructuring consumerism around freedoms of choice and freedoms of cultural expression.

Out of this came a theory and practice of what we might call "compensatory consumerism." This entailed a Faustian bargain between capital and labor in which capital said to labor: "we know we cannot create labor processes which are adequate to you, but we can compensate you so that when you come out of the labor process and go home you will have at hand a cornucopia of cheap consumer products, from which you will derive all the delirious happiness you crave. All of these consumer products will compensate for the fact that you have a miserable time at work." Out of this came the project of creating a reasonably affluent working class. The idea of compensatory consumerism became very significant and what we've seen is a huge burst since the 1970s through 1980s into new forms of consumerism. The most important thing about them was that they did not constitute mass consumption in the ordinary sense. A lot of it was niche consumption. In effect, capital responded to and in some instances created consumer niches. This produced social fragmentation and, by exploiting and in some respects shaping identity politics and culture wars, promoted lifestyle differentiations and different modes of cultural expression, sexuality, and so on.

Compensatory consumerism was seen by the corporations as one of the answers to the alienations which were being experienced in the workplace. But the problem with compensatory consumerism is that, first, it requires that the consumers have enough effective demand, have enough money, that they could go into the stores and buy all they wanted. The capitalist response was not necessarily to increase wages but to lower the cost of consumer goods. While wages remained stagnant, what those wages could buy was increasing because of the general decline in costs of consumer goods (many of which were produced in China). The material well-being of the working classes could improve even as wage levels stagnated. This was particularly true to the degree that individual wage levels stagnated but households increased their income by women joining the labor force in large numbers, in part incentivized by the enticements of consumerism and the proliferation of labor-saving household technologies and services. But here too there comes a point where it's not clear that compensatory consumerism really works.

When we look at the consumer side of what capital is about, we see that capital transforms wants, needs and desires so as to create the kind of market required for "rational consumption," rational, that is, from the standpoint of capital. But compensatory consumerism hasn't worked very well for a couple of reasons. The first is that as the 1980s wore on so the affluent working class came under attack through automation and through the revitalization of manufacturing along high-tech lines. And the "affluent worker," as he (and it was mainly masculine) was often referred to in the early 1980s, was gradually under assault, union power was being diminished by a variety of means – both political attack but also the substitution of that working class in the factories by automation so that fewer and fewer workers were required. The declining purchasing power of large segments of the population left them very much on the margins of this compensatory consumerism. Those that were incorporated in the compensatory consumerism began to have certain frustrations about the nature of the products that they were actually being offered.

There is an interesting history on the sales side. I remember reading Émile Zola's novel about the new department stores in Paris during the Second Empire. The Prefect of Paris asks the owner "how do you manage to make such a profit?" The answer came back: "get the women" as consumers, and then the men will have to pay. That was the gendered way in which it was set up. I always think about that when I go to a department store because the first things you encounter in almost all department stores are perfumes and handbags and women's products. You have to go up to the fourth floor to find the men's stuff. So, "get the women" is still important. But since 1945 there has been another line and it was "get the kids" as consumers. This form of consumerism has become even more viciously exploitative and in its own way alienating.

How satisfying has compensatory consumerism been? To begin with, a lot of the products were rather shoddy, and a lot of them fell apart. This is convenient because capital does not want products which last a long time, lest the market gets saturated. Compensatory consumerism meant creating new fashions on a daily basis if possible and making all sorts of products which do not last. This produces a dynamism in consumer markets which can become tiring and frustrating. Furthermore, many of the household technologies that are supposed to save time and labor turn out not to do that at all.

This reminds me of an interesting moment in *Capital* where Marx talks about John Stuart Mill, who wondered why it was that the new factory technologies were not lightening the load of labor but rather making the lot of the laborer worse. Marx answers that of course that's the case, because the purpose of the new technology is not to lighten the load of labor, but to increase the rate of exploitation of labor power. I feel the same way about many of the new consumerist household technologies. Every household had to have a refrigerator, a dishwasher, a washing machine, a TV, computers for video games, mobile phones, and all the rest of it. This absorbed much of the surplus productive capacity arising within the capitalist economy. But the role of these household goods and consumer durables was to create and expand a new market as short term as possible. Most products do not last. We need a new computer every three or four years and a new mobile phone every two.

There is a rapid turnover in consumption, even to the point where capital starts to cultivate forms of consumption which are pretty much instantaneous and are non-exclusionary. A lot of capital gets invested in making, say, a Netflix series, but that Netflix series can be consumed instantaneously by a vast population, and it's not exclusionary: my watching it doesn't stop somebody else watching it. The forms of consumerism start to change. Instead of making things that last a long time and which satisfy a particular need like knives, forks, and plates, and things like that, you create a vast industry of making spectacle. It's fascinating to me to suddenly look at the range of new films which get released, most of which I haven't heard of, but that absorb a large amount of capital in their production. This feeds a consumer market which is instantaneous, or very short term. You watch a Netflix episode in an hour and that's it, it's done, and that's your consumption, and then you turn to the next hour. Binge-watching consumerism takes over. Reality TV takes over even to the point where the daily news is turned into a consumer spectacle with disastrous political consequences. The whole consumer world is changing and transforming. But it is not changing and transforming in a way which necessarily is more satisfying. Compensatory consumerism can also become alienating.

For example, consider the growth of tourism: tourism is now of course a huge industry, and there are vast amounts of investment in it. Tourism means that people will visit a place and, in effect, consume the vision of that place in a day and then go to the next place and consume the vision of that. This is a particularly interesting form of instantaneous consumption. But increasingly, tourism is having all kinds of negative effects. If you want to go to some place where it is peaceful and quiet, instead you may find there are thousands of people milling around. There are so many consumer sites now that are impossible to enjoy because there are too many tourists. I recently visited Florence and I couldn't wait to get out. Its qualities had been absolutely killed by excessive tourism. Some cities are now trying to control tourism. Barcelona, for example, suffers from an excess of tourist industry. They are trying to cut back on Airbnb and hotel construction because the character of the place starts to disintegrate and it becomes less and less satisfying for visitors and unbearable for local residents. Who wants to go to a place which is beautiful to look at only to find themselves with mobs of people, milling around, eating hot dogs and hamburgers and drinking Coca-Cola?

There are these modes of consumerism which at one time seemed to offer some compensations but which are no longer satisfying. The result is widespread alienation from compensatory consumerism. The two basic elements of our lives, the daily life we lead in our place of residence and the daily work rhythm in which we are engaged, offer less and less in the way of meaningful satisfactions even as the list of fanciful possibilities proliferates. The dissatisfactions indicate that there is something wrong with the way in which our society is headed. If you ask the question: "is our society headed in a good or a bad direction?" most people would say bad. What and where are the institutions to protect us? In the same way that the length of the working day got regulated, is there some way to control the unregulated forms of both production and consumption, which now dominate society?

The political side of things has gone from bad to worse, which is why I think the question of alienation becomes more and more significant. If there are populations alienated from their daily life and potential pleasures as well as from their work, then they are likely to look for institutions and political or other means that answer to their disaffections. The rise of religion, particularly Evangelical Christianity and radical forms of Islam, is one answer to the lack of meaning in daily life and in daily work. Beyond that, of course, there is a vast well of discontent with a political process that operates as the ruling ideas of a ruling class in which the efficiency of the market and of capital is everything, while responsibility for the environment and for everything else culturally important is regarded as extraneous or irrelevant.

Situations arise in which there is alienation from labor processes, widespread alienation in relationship to contemporary consumerism, alienation in relationship to the political process, alienation in relation to many of those institutions which have traditionally helped us cope with things and given meaning to life. All of this makes for a terrifying combination. When alienated populations are just sitting there, discontented, living in a state of passive-aggressive withdrawal from the social process, unable to care for anything because everything appears meaningless, then this is a dangerous situation. In a world infused with multiple alienations, the hidden anger becomes palpable, only wanting a trigger to explode in riot, to boil over into unstructured violence.

Alienated populations are vulnerable and open to sudden and unpredictable mobilizations. This is where the question of who is to blame for the overall malaise comes to the fore. Capital which controls the ruling ideas through control over the media ensures that capital itself is the last to be blamed. There follows a quest to find others to blame, such as immigrants, lazy people, people not like me (or you), people who offend the moral code, people who do not share my religious views or something of that kind. This typically leads to a certain political instability and even to violent confrontations. This is what we now see emerging all around the world as authoritarian figures emerge from the shadows to suddenly capture the anger of the masses. "Give me your anger," these new often charismatic leaders seem to say, "and I will channel it and take you to the source of the problems." Immigrants, minorities, people of color, feminists, socialists, secularists are all lined up as scapegoats. We get, in short, the kind of politics that is now all around us. I know this is a far too simplistic representation of our current situation but I think there's a certain virtue in the crudity. Blame everyone and everything other than capital, the sacred God of our social universe. But capital has reached a terminal positionality in terms of the dynamic of accumulation and continuous exponential growth, in exploding social inequalities, in deepening debt peonage of increasing wage slavery, and rapidly deteriorating environmental conditions. The ability of people to sustain themselves through a shallow compensatory consumerism and empty gestures towards inclusion is in free fall. The frustrations are manifold. The concept of alienation has to be brought back into the political dialogue. We won't understand what is going on in politics without it. Whole populations have essentially given in to their alienated conditions.

Ways of life are failing and being abandoned, leaving in their wake drug and alcoholic addiction, opioid dependency, and the like. Life expectancies have been declining in many parts of the world, even in Britain and in many parts of the United States.

There is a general malaise in populations that feel alienated, abandoned, and neglected. They feel there is nothing possible except to cheer on and follow some charismatic leader who releases and channels their latent anger. We're seeing the emergence of extreme right-wing, populist movements all around the world. The situation in Brazil, for example, is disastrous. It's not only Bolsonaro. The society has moved very much to the right and is using these circumstances to try to re-establish the power of capital on the basis of an authoritarian, neo-fascist politics. We see the same thing going on in Hungary and Poland, we see gestures towards this in Germany and in France, we see Modi in India, Erdogan in Turkey, Sisi in Egypt, Duterte in the Philippines.

All manner of disastrous political forms are emerging. We need to examine the economic and political conditions in which they are rooted. The threatening right-wing political movements need to be cut off at their root. But that requires the creation of an alternative political economy which puts together an understanding of the root causes of their malaise. But without a revolutionary transformation and left unchecked the hegemonic social process and its associated dominant mental conceptions will take us deep into the bowels of fascist authoritarianism. The potentiality exists for tragic outcomes. While there are many elements at work in the creation of our present situation, it will be impossible to exit from our current difficulties without a thorough exploration of the structures of alienation that are currently enveloping us.

17

Alienation at Work:
The Politics of a Plant Closure

I had a very interesting weekend in Chicago recently with the artist LaToya Ruby Frazier. She has been a photographic artist for some time and is well known in cultural circles. She had decided to investigate and record the impact of the closure of the Lordstown General Motors Plant on the workers. The announcement about the closure came between Thanksgiving and Christmas 2018. It was a bit of a surprise and a shock because it seemed to many of the workers that General Motors had been doing very well. General Motors had a high rate of profit and huge resources, yet here they were closing down a plant which made the General Motors compact car, the Chevrolet Cruze. LaToya decided to go to Lordstown to get some sense of what the impact of this closure was going to be on the workers and their families.

When she got there, of course, she found that she was not welcome by General Motors. They tried to keep her out of the plant and they were even rather threatening in some of the things they said. So, she had to do her work off-site and this gave it a special coloration, because it meant that not only was she working with individual workers in the plant, but she was also involved with the families in their homes. The families in this case were going to be seriously affected. When the closure was announced, the company promised to find the workers a job elsewhere within the General Motors system. But nobody knew exactly where they might be reassigned, where they might have to go. So what followed was a period of silence. But then workers would get a letter, in which they were given four days to decide whether they wanted to transfer to a different location or whether they wanted to just get out of General

THE ANTI-CAPITALIST CHRONICLES

Motors employment altogether, in which case they would lose their benefits. They had four days to decide and they were given three weeks to move to the new location. Imagine what that meant for a family where, say, either the mother or the father was employed in the plant. This had a huge impact: do you take the whole family? Does the husband, or the wife, move? And how far away would they move? Would they be 600 miles away, 1,000 miles away?

This had a pretty draconian effect, and LaToya was witness to a wrenching decision-making process, recording the anguish it produced in families, the impact on young children (suddenly confronted with the fact that a parent would be gone to another plant, and wouldn't be seen except once every three weeks or something of that kind). Or the family as a whole might move, in which case all of their social relations and support networks would be disrupted. The need for such a rapid decision had a traumatic impact upon those concerned, and the photographic essay illuminates the trauma of this. But it does something else as well. What LaToya wanted to do was not only to give us a photographic essay and record. She also, through a series of interviews, gave voice to how the families were responding to and talking about this rather brutal treatment by the company, and what their feelings were about the whole event.

The Lordstown plant of General Motors was set up in the late 1960s. It was touted as a special experiment in industrial labor relations. In the 1960s, there was a great deal of emphasis on trying to create a labor process that was worker-friendly. There was an attempt to give workers more participatory investment in the labor process. Lordstown was set up at a moment when there was quite a lot of emphasis in the literature on something called "X-efficiency." The idea was that a less alienated labor force would be much more efficient and effective than one that was more alienated and that didn't care about its involvement in production. There was an attempt by some of the automobile companies at that time to create a new structure of labor relations, in which the compliance, and the collaboration, and the cooperation of the workers were emphasized as opposed to only their repression and their domination, as had been the norm in the capitalist factory labor process from its inception.

Now this was possible because of the particular and peculiar situation of the automobile industry during the 1960s. The industry was consolidated into three large automobile companies, General Motors, Ford, and Chrysler. The literature at the time depicted this as a classic form of monopoly capital. The three Detroit auto companies were not technically a monopoly, they were an oligopoly, just a few firms, but they engaged in price leadership, and they were generally seen as being dominant in the US economy. At that time there were no foreign firms around: there was no Toyota, no Volkswagen, BMW, or anything like that to challenge them. In the literature at the time, if you read Sweezy and Baran's *Monopoly Capital*, the Detroit auto companies were seen as a good example of how monopoly capital really worked, which was by price collaboration, price leadership, and price fixing. This gave the auto companies a certain amount of leeway to negotiate with the unions.

As the auto workers' union became strong during the 1950s and 1960s, there arose a process of what's called "panel bargaining." The auto workers would, in effect, pick one of the auto companies and say: "Okay, let's renegotiate our contract, insert certain things, such as cost of living clauses, which said that wages would increase as the cost of living increased, things of that sort." If auto workers successfully organized a contract with Ford, then they would go to the other auto companies and say: "Hey, this is what Ford did, we expect you to do something roughly the same." The other auto companies would follow suit, but not exactly, so they could avoid conflict with the anti-trust legislation, and say they were in competition. But in practice they were not competing that much and the workers could expect reasonably favorable and compatible contracts. I say "reasonably favorable" in a very qualified sense, because there was always a lot of struggle, always a lot of fighting, on shop floor conditions, on wage rates, on the employment of minorities, and there were strong movements within the auto workers. For example, the Revolutionary Union Movements of Detroit, and later the League of Revolutionary Black Workers, were actually pushing the auto companies even further than was possible at that time.

In the 1960s then, there was a corporate interest in trying to collaborate with the workers, and bring the workers on board, to govern not only by coercion, but also by consent. And the consent involved worker control over certain aspects of the labor process: assignments of tasks, and things of that kind. Lordstown was created as an innovative labor process from the standpoint of capital, in which consent was emphasized. The labor force of Lordstown had a special relationship to the company. This marked Lordstown as a special branch of General Motors. Interestingly, the Lordstown experiment seems to have failed in its immediate objectives for a very interesting reason. The evidence suggests that the auto companies were right to say that once workers became involved in the design and assignments in the labor process, the workers were likely to become much more involved, and therefore much more efficient and proud of their situation and their product. Labor was less alienated. But this also meant that workers were involved in determining the conditions of their own production, and once engaged they wanted to determine more. Lordstown became a center of worker militancy, precisely because of the advanced consciousness and engagement of the workers. The workers were conscious of who was in charge, and to the degree that they felt slightly empowered, they began to think even more about what that empowerment might mean. So Lordstown, which was supposed to be a model of collaborative endeavor, became a site of militant struggle.

What LaToya found was that the tradition of pride in the production process and pride in their membership of this plant never went away. For this reason, the closure of the plant came as a double shock. It wasn't simply that the plant closed down, it was that a way of life and a way of being was suddenly challenged. The closure was traumatic at all kinds of levels. It disrupted family life and social relations. It was the loss of engagement in a production process in which people had a certain pride and to the degree that the workers felt pride in the excellence of their work and their product, it became doubly hard to accept the fact of closure. Interestingly, the closure has in part to be ascribed to the incoherence of Trump's economic policies. Trump had promised to help blue-collar manufacturing workers. But one of the reasons that the Lordstown plant had been kept open was because there was a regulation that prevented the major auto companies concentrating their production on SUVs, which were economically successful, and not bothering about the production of more environmentally friendly but less economically successful compact cars.

The Lordstown plant was producing the General Motors compact car – the Cruze – as the regulations required. But when Trump abolished the regulation, General Motors didn't have to produce compact cars anymore. Trump, in his anti-environmentalist passion to deregulate, abolished the regulation which was preserving employment in Lordstown. The loss of jobs in Lordstown was, therefore, partially Trump's doing.

Another important part of this history was that the oligopolistic structure of the big three Detroit auto companies had been protected against foreign competition during the 1960s because the Bretton-Woods international system was founded on capital controls. This meant that capital couldn't move freely into or out of the United States. Of course, this isn't to say that there was no capital movement going on, but that the different nation states were really protected territories within which quasi-monopolies could form. The protected territory of the United States made it possible for the big three auto makers to dominate. But capital controls were, for a number of reasons, abandoned in 1971. The effect was to open up the US market to foreign capital and this allowed foreign auto companies to enter into the United States and compete with the Detroit oligopoly. In the late 1970s and early 1980s, there was a huge wave of investment in which the Japanese and German auto companies came in. The monopoly power of Detroit was broken particularly with respect to the compact car market. The Japanese had a better and cheaper product.

Suddenly in the 1980s, Detroit found itself in economic difficulty vis-à-vis stiff foreign competition. Detroit abandoned its collaborative strategies with the auto workers, and moved to a more coercive strategy, which it began to do in the 1970s and 1980s. But implementing a more coercive strategy at Lordstown, where there is a class-conscious and militant labor force, meant that there was a great deal of struggle going on in Lordstown. The labor relations literature of the late 1960s and early 1970s talked about worker circles and production circles in the automobile industry, which also had some support from the US Department of Labor, but by the late 1970s and early1980s the literature abandons all of that. The message became: "We have to put the working class back into its box, and we have to start to create labor systems which are far more coercive." The result was for capital to view the labor force as a disposable labor force which can easily be thrown to one side, and so there is a real transformation in labor relations in the plants.

But then comes the crisis of 2007–08 which created acute difficulties for the auto companies. The consumer power in the United States collapsed during the housing crisis. Seven million households lost their houses, which meant they're not buying new cars. General Motors nearly went bankrupt. In fact, it technically did go bankrupt, it had to be bailed out. In effect, General Motors was nationalized for a brief period, taken over by the state, and bailed out by the state. It was also rescued by the auto workers who agreed to renegotiate their contracts. This was an important moment. The auto workers in effect saved their own jobs by saving the firm that employed them. They could only do this by reducing their wage demands and their access to benefits: healthcare and pensions. An agreement was reached with the union, which introduced a two-tiered labor force. The older workers who had been there under standard contracts would keep their privileges in terms of both the wage rate, but even more important, to healthcare and to pension rights. Newer hires within General Motors went on to the second tier, which didn't have the same wage rate, pension rights, and healthcare. So you had two people working side by side doing the same job in the same plant, but under different contractual conditions. In effect, old labor, which had seniority, was kept on the old system, while young people coming on had to accept the conditions of the new contract, which were much reduced. The dual effect of state intervention and of labor union concessions rescued General Motors from the difficulties of

2007–08 step by step to the point that, right now, it is one of the most profitable companies in the country.

The workers themselves frequently said in their conversations with LaToya that they couldn't understand why the Lordstown plant was to be closed when they had given so generously, given up many of their hard-won former gains to rescue the company. The company was now incredibly profitable, and in this very moment the company suddenly turns around and treats them as disposable nothings instead of a loyal workforce that had sacrificed to save the company. Furthermore, it seemed particularly cruel to give them four days to decide if they would transfer to another plant in Missouri, Minnesota, or wherever. And here is the kicker: if they didn't accept transfer, they lost all their benefits. Now, imagine what stress that ultimatum creates. If you've got pension benefits and healthcare benefits for a family, and suddenly you're faced with the fact that if you don't accept transfer to some plant that is 600 or 1,000 miles away, you're going to lose all of that. What do you do, and how do you do it, and how do you discuss it? And you only have four days to discuss it and decide. This is absolutely unconscionable to me, but it shows you the state of labor relations in one of the more privileged sectors of union bargaining, and what that might mean for the working population as a whole. Some people decided that they could not accept their offer, and they would just have to take the consequences. This entailed a real reduction in living standards, in their security, but, if it meant that they would have to break up the family, many preferred to preserve those valued social relations in the community.

This, I think, emphasizes something about the way the labor process is viewed from the standpoint of capital. Labor is simply a use value, a factor of production, which is disposable, and which can be had under certain circumstances and legal possibilities. That's all it is, whereas to the worker, of course, it's all about family life and social relations, it's about what's on the shop floor as well as in the community, it's about how everything works and relates together, the role of the union, and union employees, and the like. This is important to look at because right now the emphasis in capitalist corporations is on efficiency and the profit rate. Nothing else really matters. There is no corporate responsibility for conditions of life in the community, when General Motors and the union had both been deeply enmeshed in the community life.

For instance, United Way, which is a big institution for charitable giving, has had a large presence through funding a lot of community services, cultural activities, social welfare structures, and so on. The United Way contribution that came from the General Motors employees was huge. The company matched the employees' contributions dollar for dollar. If the employees gave $100,000, then the company would put in another $100,000. But with the closure this was all going to disappear. The community had been knitted together through charitable giving and, obviously, if people have no longer any employment in General Motors, they're not going to be able to give. The community faces a serious erosion of its social fabric, and of its social relations, and its capacity for social and cultural provision.

In the history of capital, firms grow and some collapse. We know that happens. It is not as if we would say that under no circumstances should you ever close a plant. The big questions are: how do you do it and why do you do it? In the General Motors' case, the rhetoric of the CEO Mary Barra has been to re-emphasize how the General Motors community is all one big family, at the very moment when it is destroying families left, right and center.

But there is a new direction emerging for General Motors, which is electric-powered vehicles. So now General Motors is saying that in the future it doesn't want to be an auto company, it really wants to be a high-tech company. General Motors is trying to take a page out of Tesla's book, and say we're going into the production of electric cars. There is a real problem with the automobile industry. It contributes mightily to pollution and to climate change. We clearly need to transition from the automobile and fossil fuel usage in general. There is a lot of surplus capacity in automobile production worldwide, particularly in traditional forms of automobile production. This makes no sense. The main economic base of São Paulo is in the automobile industry at the same time as the city is notorious for its traffic jams and its poor air quality. There has to be some sort of planning, some sort of reorganization of social order so that we transition away from mass automobile production. I'm not going to say that the Lordstown plant should be kept open indefinitely. We have to recognize that, at a certain point, we would want to live in a society where we are not so dependent on automobiles, and that would mean that the economic base of the society would have to change. But it's one thing to say that, and another to come up with a transition plan over 15 or 20 years, and take the social structures which are there in Lordstown, and the skills which are available there, and transition into something different. There is only one way to think about this, and that's by some sort of coherent plan of reassignment and reconstruction of the automobile industry into something different. I don't really worry too much when somebody says we should think about transitioning from automobile production to high-tech production of electric artificial intelligence vehicular systems. I'm okay with that, and I think we should all be okay with that. What has been so objectionable about the Lordstown experience is the way in which it treats workers as disposable items to be cast off or thrown away as profitability demands.

Furthermore, it throws away all of the community and in many instances communal resources which had been built up in terms of social relations, structures of social provision, and the like. There has to be some way in which we can do these transitions better, and that way is of course one which capital would almost certainly not want to embrace. The capitalists continue to operate in the same way. General Motors owes no loyalty to its workers. It owes everything to the stockholders and the CEOs. In the name of assuring high dividends and exorbitant salaries to its CEOs, it destroys a viable workforce, a community and whole structures of social relations, leaving nothing behind except terrifying possibilities. Ohio is a place where the opioid epidemic rages, based upon unemployment, the loss of identity and meaning, and, yes, upon a deepening alienation. This is what is ravaging communities in Ohio.

We have to come up with something which doesn't impose the social costs of sudden closure, without any consultation with the union, without any kind of discussion with communal organizations. General Motors was willing to have conversations with its union when they were in trouble, but now they are flush they don't need those conversations anymore. This is what allows them to treat their ex-workers as disposable dirt which doesn't belong in their vision of what the future should be. LaToya's wonderful photographic essay and the written commentaries of the workers and their families highlight an unnecessary tragedy in the making. This is the kind of story that should turn everyone resolutely towards anti-capitalism as the only possible political posture.

18

Anti-Capitalist Politics
in the Time of COVID-19

When trying to interpret, understand, and analyze the daily flow of news, I tend to locate what is happening against the background of two distinctive but intersecting models of how capitalism works. The first level is a mapping of the internal contradictions of the circulation and accumulation of capital as money value flows in search of profit through the different "moments" (as Marx calls them) of production, realization (consumption), distribution, and reinvestment. This is a model of the capitalist economy as a spiral of endless expansion and growth. It gets pretty complicated as it gets elaborated through, for example, the lenses of geopolitical rivalries, uneven geographical developments, financial institutions, state policies, technological reconfigurations, and the ever-changing web of divisions of labor and of social relations.

I envision this model as embedded, however, in a broader context of social reproduction (in households and communities), in an ongoing and ever-evolving metabolic relation to nature (including the "second nature" of urbanization and the built environment) and all manner of cultural, scientific (knowledge-based), religious, and contingent social formations that human populations typically create across space and time. These latter "moments" incorporate the active expression of human wants, needs and desires, the lust for knowledge and meaning, and the evolving quest for fulfillment against a background of changing institutional arrangements, political contestations, ideological confrontations, losses, defeats, frustrations and alienations, all worked out in a world of marked geographical, cultural, social, and political diversity. This second model constitutes, as it were, my working understanding of global capitalism as a distinctive social formation, whereas the first is about the contradictions within the economic engine that powers this social formation along certain pathways of its historical and geographical evolution.

When on 26 January, 2020 I first read of a coronavirus that was gaining ground in China, I immediately thought of the repercussions for the global dynamics of capital accumulation. I knew from my studies of the economic model that blockages and disruptions in the continuity of capital flow would result in devaluations and that if devaluations became widespread and deep that would signal the onset of crises. I was also well aware that China is the second largest economy in the world and that it had effectively bailed out global capitalism in the aftermath of 2007–08, so any hit upon China's economy was bound to have serious consequences for a global economy that was in any case already in a parlous condition. The existing model of capital accumulation was, it seemed to me, already in a lot of trouble. Protest movements were occurring almost everywhere (from Santiago to Beirut), many of which were focused on the fact that the dominant economic model was not working well for the mass of the population. This neoliberal model is increasingly resting on fictitious capital and a vast expansion in the money supply and debt creation. It is already facing the problem of insufficient effective demand to realize the values that capital is capable of producing. How might the dominant economic model, with its sagging legitimacy and delicate health, absorb and survive the inevitable impacts of what has become a pandemic? The answer depends heavily on how long the disruption might last and spread, for as Marx pointed out, devaluation does not occur because commodities cannot be sold but because they cannot be sold in time.

I had long refused the idea of "nature" as outside of and separate from culture, economy, and daily life. I take a more dialectical and relational view of the metabolic relation to nature. Capital modifies the environmental conditions of its own reproduction but does so in a context of unintended consequences (like climate change) and against the background of autonomous and independent evolutionary forces that are perpetually re-shaping environmental conditions. There is, from this standpoint, no such thing as a truly natural disaster. Viruses mutate all of the time to be sure. But the circumstances in which a mutation becomes life-threatening depend on human actions. There are two relevant aspects to this. First, favorable environmental conditions increase the probability of vigorous mutations. It is plausible to expect that rapid transformation of habitat and intensive or wayward food supply systems in, for example, the humid sub-tropics may contribute to this. Such systems exist in many places, including China south of the Yangtze and Southeast Asia. Second, the conditions that favor rapid transmission through host bodies vary greatly. High density human populations would seem an easy host target. It is well known that measles epidemics, for example, only flourish in larger urban population centers but rapidly die out in sparsely populated regions. How human beings interact with each other, move around, discipline themselves, or forget to wash their hands affect how diseases get transmitted. In recent times, SARS, Bird and Swine Flu appear to have come out of China or Southeast Asia. China has suffered heavily also from swine fever in the past year, entailing the mass slaughter of pigs and escalating pork prices. I do not say all this to indict China. There are plenty of other places where environmental risks for viral mutation and diffusion are high. The Spanish Flu of 1918 may have come out of Kansas and Africa may have incubated HIV/AIDS and certainly initiated West Nile and Ebola, while dengue seems to flourish in Latin America. But the economic and demographic impacts of the spread of the virus depend upon pre-existing cracks and vulnerabilities in the hegemonic economic model.

I was not unduly surprised that COVID-19 was initially found in Wuhan (though whether it originated there is not known). Plainly the local effects would be substantial and given this was a serious production center there would likely be global economic repercussions (though I had no idea of the magnitude). The big question was how the contagion and diffusion might occur and how long it would last (until a vaccine could be found). Earlier experience had shown that one of the downsides of increasing globalization is how impossible it is to stop a rapid international diffusion of new diseases. We live in a highly connected world where almost everyone travels. The human networks for potential diffusion are vast and open. The danger (economic and demographic) was that the disruption would last a year or more.

While there was an immediate downturn in global stock markets when the initial news broke, it was surprisingly followed by a month or more when the markets hit new highs. The news seemed to indicate business as normal everywhere except in China. The belief seemed to be that we were going to experience a re-run of SARS which turned out to be fairly quickly contained and of low global impact even though it had a high death rate and created an unnecessary (in retrospect) panic in financial markets. When COVID-19 appeared, a dominant reaction was to depict it as a SARS repeat rendering the panic redundant. The fact that the epidemic raged in China, which quickly and ruthlessly moved to contain its impacts, also led the rest of the world to erroneously treat the problem as something going on "over there" and therefore out of sight and mind (accompanied by some troubling signs of anti-Chinese xenophobia in certain parts of the world). The spike which the virus put into the otherwise triumphant China growth story was even greeted with glee in certain circles of the Trump administration. However, stories of interruptions in global production chains that passed through Wuhan began to circulate. These were largely ignored or treated as problems for particular product lines or corporations (like Apple). Devaluations were local and particular and not systemic. The signs of falling consumer demand were also minimized, even though those corporations, like McDonalds and Starbucks, that had large operations inside the Chinese domestic market had to close their doors there for a while. The overlap of the Chinese New Year with the outbreak of the virus masked impacts throughout January. The complacency of this response was badly misplaced.

Initial news of the international spread of the virus was occasional and episodic with a serious outbreak in South Korea and a few other hotspots like Iran. It was the Italian outbreak that sparked the first violent reaction. The stock market crash beginning in mid-February oscillated somewhat but by mid-March had led to a net devaluation of almost 30 percent on stock markets worldwide. The exponential escalation of the infections elicited a range of often incoherent and sometimes panic-stricken responses. President Trump performed an imitation of King Canute in the face of a potential rising tide of illnesses and deaths. Some of the responses have been passing strange. Having the Federal Reserve lower interest rates in the face of a virus seemed weird, even when it was recognized that the move was meant to alleviate market impacts rather than to stem the progress of the virus.

Public authorities and healthcare systems were almost everywhere caught short-handed. Forty years of neoliberalism across North and South America and Europe had left the public totally exposed and ill-prepared to face a public health crisis of this sort, even though previous scares of SARS and Ebola provided abundant warnings as well as cogent lessons as to what should be done. In many parts of the supposed "civilized" world, local governments and regional/state authorities, which invariably form the front line of defense in public health and safety emergencies of this kind, had been starved of funding thanks to a policy of austerity designed to fund tax cuts and subsidies to the corporations and the rich. Corporatist Big Pharma has little or no interest in non-remunerative research on infectious diseases (such as the whole class of coronaviruses that have been well known since the 1960s). Big Pharma rarely invests in prevention. It has little interest in investing in preparedness for a public health crisis. It loves to design cures. The sicker we are, the more they earn. Prevention does not contribute to shareholder value. It might even diminish it. The business model applied to public health provision eliminated the surplus coping capacities that would be required in an emergency. Prevention was not even an enticing enough field of work to warrant public private partnerships. President Trump had cut the budget of the Centers for Disease Control and disbanded the working group on pandemics in the National Security Council in the same spirit as he cut all research funding, including on climate change. If I wanted to be anthropomorphic and metaphorical about this, I would conclude that COVID-19 is Nature's revenge for over forty years of Nature's gross and abusive mistreatment at the hands of a violent and unregulated neoliberal extractivism.

It is perhaps symptomatic that the least neoliberal countries, China and South Korea, Taiwan and Singapore, have so far come through the pandemic in better shape than Italy, though Iran will bely this argument as a universal principle. While there was a lot of evidence that China handled SARS rather badly with a lot of initial dissembling and denial, this time around President Xi moved to mandate transparency both in reporting and testing as did South Korea. Even so, in China valuable time was lost (just a few days make all the difference). What was remarkable in China, however, was the confinement of the epidemic to Hubei Province with Wuhan at its center. The epidemic did not move with the same ferocity to Beijing or to the west or even further south. By the end of March, China announced no new cases in Hubei and Volvo announced it was returning car production to normal when the rest of the global auto industry was shutting down. The measures taken to confine the virus geographically were comprehensive and restrictive (as they had to be). They would be difficult to replicate elsewhere for political, economic, and cultural reasons. Reports coming out of China suggest the treatments and the policies were anything but caring. Furthermore, China and Singapore deployed their powers of personal surveillance to levels that were invasive and authoritarian. But they seem to have been extremely effective in aggregate, though had the counter actions been set in motion just a few days earlier, models suggest that many deaths might have been avoided. This is important information: in any exponential growth process there is an inflexion point beyond which the rising mass gets totally out of control (note here, once more, the significance of the mass in relation to the rate). The fact that Trump dawdled for so many weeks will almost certainly prove costly in human lives.

The economic effects are now spiraling out of control across the globe. The disruptions working through the value chains of corporations and in certain sectors turned out to be more systemic and substantial than was originally thought. The long-term effect may be to shorten or diversify the supply chains while moving towards less labor-intensive forms of production (with enormous implications for employment) and greater reliance on artificial intelligent production systems. The disruption of production chains entails laying off or furloughing workers, which diminishes final demand, while the demand for raw materials diminishes productive consumption. These impacts on the demand side would in their own right have produced at least a mild recession.

But the biggest vulnerabilities existed elsewhere. The modes of consumerism which exploded after 2007–08 have crashed with devastating consequences. These modes were based on reducing the turnover time of consumption as close as possible to zero. The flood of investments into such forms of consumerism had everything to do with maximum absorption of exponentially increasing volumes of capital in forms of consumerism that had the shortest possible turnover time. International tourism was emblematic. International visits increased from 800 million to 1.4 billion between 2010 and 2018. This form of instantaneous "experiential" consumerism required massive infrastructural investments in airports and airlines, hotels and restaurants, theme parks and cultural events, and so on. This site of capital accumulation is now dead in the water, airlines are close to bankruptcy, hotels are empty and mass unemployment in the hospitality industries is imminent. Eating out is not a good idea and restaurants and bars have been closed in many places. Even take-out appears risky. The vast army of workers in the gig economy or in other forms of precarious work is being laid off with no visible means of support. Events such as cultural festivals, soccer and basketball tournaments, concerts, business and professional conventions, and even political gatherings around elections are cancelled. These "event-based" forms of experiential consumerism have been closed down. The revenues of local governments have cratered. Universities and schools are closing down.

Much of the cutting-edge model of contemporary capitalist consumerism is inoperable under present conditions. The drive towards what André Gorz describes as "compensatory consumerism" (in which alienated workers are supposed to recover their spirits through a package holiday on a tropical beach) was blunted.

But contemporary capitalist economies are 70 or even 80 percent driven by consumerism. Consumer confidence and sentiment has over the past forty years become the key to the mobilization of effective demand and capital has become increasingly demand and needs driven. This source of economic energy has not been subject to wild fluctuations (with a few exceptions such as the Icelandic volcanic eruption that blocked transatlantic flights for a couple of weeks). But COVID-19 is underpinning not a wild fluctuation but an almighty crash in the heart of the form of consumerism that dominates in the most affluent countries. The spiral form of endless capital accumulation is collapsing inward from one part of the world to every other. The only thing that can save it is a government-funded and inspired mass consumerism conjured out of nothing. This will require socializing the whole of the economy in the United States, for example, without calling it socialism. Whatever else happens, the widespread popular skepticism as to the need for a government armed with wide powers has been put to rest and the difference between good and bad administrations is being more widely acknowledged. Having governments subservient to the interests of the bond-holders and the financiers (as has been the case since 2007–08) is turning out to be a bad idea, even for the financiers.

There is a convenient myth that infectious diseases do not acknowledge class or other social barriers and boundaries. Like many such sayings, there is a certain truth to this. In the cholera epidemics of the nineteenth century, the transcendence of barriers of class was sufficiently dramatic as to spawn the birth of a public sanitation and health movement (which became professionalized) that has lasted to this day. Whether this movement was designed to protect everyone or just the upper classes was not always clear. But today the differential class and social effects and impacts tell a different story. The economic and social impacts are filtered through "customary" discriminations that are everywhere in evidence. To begin with, the workforce that is expected to take care of the mounting numbers of the sick is typically highly gendered, racialized, and ethnicized in most parts of the world. It mirrors the class-based workforces to be found in, for example, airports and other logistical sectors.

This "new working class" is in the forefront and bears the brunt of either being the workforce most at risk from contracting the virus through their jobs or of being laid off with no resources because of the economic retrenchment enforced by the virus. There is, for example, the question of who can work at home and who cannot. This sharpens the societal divide as does the question of who can afford to isolate or quarantine themselves (with or without pay) in the event of contact or infection. In exactly the same way that I learned to call the Nicaraguan (1972) and Mexico City (1985) earthquakes "class-quakes" so the progress of COVID-19 exhibits all the characteristics of a class, gendered, and racialized pandemic. While efforts at mitigation are conveniently cloaked in the rhetoric that "we are all in this together," the practices, particularly on the part of national governments, suggest more sinister motivations. The contemporary working class in the United States (comprised predominantly of African Americans, Latinx, and waged women) faces the ugly choice of contamination in the name of caring and keeping key features of provision (like grocery stores) open or unemployment with no benefits (such as adequate healthcare). Salaried personnel (like me) work from home and draw their pay just as before while CEOs fly around in private jets and helicopters.

Workforces in most parts of the world have long been socialized to behave as good neoliberal subjects (which means blaming themselves or God if anything goes wrong but never daring to suggest capitalism might be the problem). But even good neoliberal subjects can see that there is something wrong with the way this pandemic is being responded to.

The big question is how long will this go on? It could be more than a year and the longer it goes on, the more the devaluation including of the labor force. Unemployment levels will almost certainly rise to levels comparable to the 1930s in the absence of massive state interventions that will have to go against the neoliberal grain. The immediate ramifications for the economy as well as for social daily life are multiple. But they are not all bad. To the degree that contemporary consumerism was becoming excessive it was verging on what Marx described as "over-consumption and insane consumption, signifying, by its turn to the monstrous and the bizarre, the downfall" of the whole system. The recklessness of this over-consumption has played a major role in environmental degradation. The cancellation of airline flights and radical curbing of transportation and movement has had positive consequence with respect to greenhouse gas emissions. Air quality in Wuhan is much improved as it also is in many US cities. Ecotourist sites will have a time to recover from trampling feet. The swans have returned to the canals of Venice. To the degree that the taste for reckless and senseless overconsumerism is curbed there could be some long-term benefits. Fewer deaths on Mount Everest could be a good thing. And while no one says it out loud, the demographic bias of the virus may end up affecting age pyramids with long-term effects on social security burdens and the future of the "care industry." Daily life will slow down and for some people that will be a blessing. The suggested rules of social distancing could, if the emergency goes on long enough, lead to cultural shifts. The only form of experiential consumerism that will almost certainly benefit is what I call the "Netflix" economy, which caters to "binge watchers" anyway.

On the economic front responses have been conditioned by the manner of exodus from the crash of 2007–08. This entailed an ultra-loose monetary policy coupled with bailing out the banks supplemented by a dramatic increase in productive consumption by a massive expansion of infrastructural investment in China. The latter cannot be repeated on the scale required. The bail-out packages set up in 2008 focused on the banks but also entailed the de facto nationalization of General Motors. It is perhaps significant that in the face of worker discontents and collapsing market demand, the three big Detroit auto companies are closing down at least temporarily. If China cannot repeat its 2007–08 role, then the burden of exiting from the current economic crisis now shifts to the United States and here is the ultimate irony: the only policies that will work, both economically and politically, are far more socialistic than anything that Bernie Sanders might propose and these rescue programs will have to be initiated under the aegis of Donald Trump, presumably under the mask of Making America Great Again. All those Republicans who so viscerally opposed the 2008 bail-out will have to eat crow or defy Donald Trump. The latter will likely cancel the elections on an emergency basis and declare the origin of an imperial presidency to save capital and the world from riot and revolution. If the only policies that will work are socialist, then the ruling oligarchy will doubtless move to ensure they be national socialist rather than people socialist. The task of anti-capitalist politics is to prevent this from happening.

19

The Collective Response
to a Collective Dilemma

I write this in the midst of the corona crisis in New York City. It is a difficult time to know exactly how to respond to what is happening. Normally in a situation of this kind, we anti-capitalists would be out on the streets demonstrating and agitating. Instead, I am in a frustrating situation of personal isolation at a moment when the time calls for collective forms of action. But as Marx famously put it, we cannot make history under circumstance of our own choosing. So we have to figure out how best to make use of the opportunities we do have.

My own circumstances are relatively privileged. I can continue to work but from home. I have not lost my job and I still get paid. All I have to do is to hide away from the virus. My age and gender put me in the vulnerable category, so no contact is advised. This gives me plenty of time to reflect and write in between zoom sessions. But rather than dwelling upon the particularities of the situation here in New York, I thought I might offer some reflections on possible alternatives and ask: how does an anti-capitalist think about circumstances of this kind?

I begin with a commentary that Marx makes on what happened in the failed revolutionary movement of the Paris Commune of 1871. Marx writes:

The working class did not expect miracles from the commune. They have no ready-made utopias to introduce by decree of the people. They know in order to work out their own emancipation and along with it that higher form to which present society is irresistibly trending by its own economical agencies, they will have to pass through long struggles, through a series of historic processes transforming circumstances and men. They have no ideals to realize but to set free the elements of the new society with which old collapsing bourgeois society itself is pregnant.

Let me make some comments on this passage. First, of course, Marx was antagonistic somewhat to the thinking of the socialist utopians, of which there were many in the 1840s, 1850s, and 1860s in France. This was the tradition of Fourier, Saint-Simon, Cabet, Blanqui, Proudhon, and so on. Marx felt that the utopian socialists were dreamers and that they were not practical workers who were going to actually transform the conditions of labor in the here and now. In order to transform conditions here and now you needed a good grasp on exactly what the nature of capitalist society is about. But Marx is very clear that the revolutionary project must concentrate on the self-emancipation of the workers. The "self" part of this formulation is important. Any major project to change the world will require also a transformation of the self. So workers would have to change themselves too. This was very much on Marx's mind at the time of the Paris Commune. But he also notes that capital itself is actually creating the possibilities for transformation and that through long struggles it would be possible to "set free" the lineaments of a new society in which the workers could be released from alienated labor. The revolutionary task was to set free the elements of this new society already existing within the womb of an old collapsing bourgeois social order.

Now, let's agree that we're living in a situation of an old collapsing bourgeois society. Clearly, it's pregnant with all kinds of ugly things (like racism and xenophobia) that I do not particularly want to see set free. But Marx is not saying set free all and everything inside of that old and awful collapsing social order. What he's saying is that we need to select those aspects of the collapsing bourgeois society which will contribute to the emancipation of the workers and the working classes. This poses the question of what are those possibilities and where are they coming from? Marx does not explain that in his pamphlet on the Commune but much of his earlier theoretical work had been dedicated to revealing exactly what the constructive possibilities for the working classes might be. One of his writings where he does this at great length is in this very large, complex, and unfinished text called the *Grundrisse* which he wrote in the crisis years of 1857–58. Some passages in that work shed light on exactly what it is that Marx might have had in mind in his defense of the Paris Commune. The idea of "setting free" relates to an understanding of what was then going on inside of a bourgeois capitalist society. This is what Marx was perpetually struggling to understand.

In the *Grundrisse*, Marx dwells at length upon the question of technological change and the inherent technological dynamism of capitalism. What he shows is that capitalist society, by definition, is going to be heavily invested in innovation and heavily invested in the construction of new technological and organizational possibilities. And that is so because as an individual capitalist, if I'm in competition with other capitalists, I will get an excess profit if my technology is superior to that of my rivals. Thus, every individual capitalist has an incentive to search out a more productive technology than those with which that capitalist is competing. For this reason, technological dynamism is embedded within the heart of a capitalist society. Marx recognized this from the *Communist Manifesto* (written in 1848) onwards. This is one of the prime forces that explains the permanently revolutionary character of capitalism. It will never rest content with its existing technology. It will constantly seek to improve it because it will always reward the person, the firm, or the society that has the more advanced technology. The state, the nation, or the power bloc that possesses the most sophisticated and dynamic technology is the one that is going to lead the pack. So technological dynamism is built into the global structures of capitalism. And it has been so since its very beginnings.

Marx's perspective on this is both illuminating and interesting. When we imagine the process of technological innovation we typically think of somebody making something or other who seeks out a technological improvement in what it is that they're making. That is, the technological dynamism is specific to a particular factory, a particular production system, a particular situation. But it turns out that many technologies actually spill over from one sphere of production to another. They become generic. For instance, computer technology is available to anybody who wants to use it for whatever purposes. Automating technologies are available to all kinds of people and industries. Marx notices that by the time you get to the 1820s, 1830s, and 1840s in Britain, the invention of new technologies had already become an independent and free-standing business. That is, it's no longer somebody who's making textiles or something like that who is interested in the new technology that will increase the productivity of the labor they employ. Instead, entrepreneurs come up with a new technology that can be used all over the place. The prime initial example of this in Marx's time was the steam engine. It had all of these applications from drainage of water out of the coal mines to making steam engines and building railroads while also being applied to the power looms in the textile factories. So if you wanted to go into the business of innovation then engineering and the machine tool industry were good places to start and whole economies, such as that which arose around the city of Birmingham which specialized in machine tool making, became oriented to the production of not only new technologies but new products. Technological innovation even by Marx's time had become a free-standing business in its own right.

In the *Grundrisse*, Marx explores in detail what happens when technology becomes a business, when innovation creates new markets rather than functioning as a response to a specific existing market demand for a new technology. New technologies then become a cutting edge of the dynamism of a capitalist society. The consequences are wide-ranging. One obvious result is that technologies are never static, they're never settled and quickly become obsolete. Catching up with the latest technology can be stressful and costly. Accelerating obsolescence can be disastrous for existing firms. Nevertheless, whole sectors of society – electronics, pharmaceuticals, bio-engineering, and the like – are given over to creating innovations for the sake of innovation. Whoever can create the innovation that is going to capture the imagination (like the cell phone or the tablet) or have the most applications (like the computer chip) is likely to win out. So this idea that technology itself becomes a business becomes absolutely central in Marx's account of what a capitalist society is about. This is what differentiates capitalism from all other modes of production. The capacity to innovate has been omnipresent in human history. There were technological changes in ancient China and even under feudalism. But what becomes unique within a capitalist mode of production is the simple fact that technology becomes a business with a generic product that is sold to producers and consumers alike. This is very specific to capitalism. This becomes one of the key drivers of how capitalist society evolves. This is the world we live in whether we like it or not.

Marx goes on to point out a very significant corollary of this development. In order for technology to become a business you need to mobilize new knowledges in certain kinds of ways. This entails the application of science and technology as distinctive forms of knowledge and understandings of the world. The creation of new technologies on the ground becomes integrated with the rise of science and technology as intellectual and academic disciplines. Marx notices how the application of science and technology and the creation of new knowledges become necessary to this revolutionary technology. This defines another aspect of the nature of a capitalist mode of production. Technological dynamism is connected to a dynamism in the production of new scientific and technical knowledges and new, often revolutionary mental conceptions of the world. The fields of science and technology mesh with the production and mobilization of new knowledges and understandings. Eventually wholly new institutions, like MIT and Cal Tech were founded to facilitate this development.

Marx then goes on to ask: what does this do to the production processes within capitalism and how does it affect the way in which labor (and the worker) is incorporated into these production processes? In the pre-capitalist era, say the fifteenth, sixteenth centuries, the laborer generally had control of the means of production (the tools) and became skilled in the utilization of these tools. The skilled laborer became a monopolist of a certain kind of knowledge and certain kind of understanding which, Marx notes, was always considered an art. But by the time you get to the factory system and even more so by the time you get to the contemporary world, then that is no longer the case. The laborers' traditional skills are rendered redundant because technology and science take over and technology and science and new forms of knowledge are incorporated in the machine. The art disappears. And so Marx, in an astonishing set of passages in the *Grundrisse* (pages 650 to 710 of the Penguin edition if you are interested), talks about the way in which new technologies and knowledge become embedded in the machine; that they're no longer in the laborer's brain and the laborer is pushed to one side to become an appendage of the machine, a mere machine-minder. All of the intelligence and all of the knowledge, which used to belong to the laborers and conferred upon them a certain monopoly power vis-à-vis capital, disappear. The capitalist who once needed the skills of the laborer is freed from that constraint and the skill is now embodied in the machine. The knowledge produced through science and technology flows into the machine and the machine becomes "the soul" of capitalist dynamism. This is the situation that Marx is describing.

So the dynamism of a capitalist society becomes crucially dependent upon perpetual innovations driven by the mobilization of science and technology through the business of perpetual innovations. Marx saw this clearly in his own time. He was writing about all of this in 1858! But right now, of course, we're in a situation in which this issue has become critical and crucial. The question of artificial intelligence is the contemporary versions of what Marx was talking about. We now need to know to what degree artificial intelligence is being developed through science and technology and to what degree is it being applied and likely to be applied in production processes. The obvious effect would be to displace the laborer and in fact disarm and devalue the laborer even further in terms of the laborer's capacity for the application of imagination, skill, and expertise within the production process.

This leads Marx to make the following commentary in the *Grundrisse*. Let me cite it to you because I think it's really, really fascinating.

The transformation of the production process from the simple labor process into a scientific process, which subjugates the forces of nature and compels them to work in the service of human needs, appears as a quality of *fixed capital* in contrast to living labor ... Thus all powers of labor are transposed into powers of capital.

The knowledge and scientific expertise now lies within the machine under the command of the capitalist. The productive power of labor is relocated into the fixed capital, something which is external to labor. The laborer is pushed to one side. So fixed capital becomes the bearer of our collective knowledge and intelligence when it comes to production and consumption.

Further on, Marx homes in on what it is that the collapsing bourgeois order is pregnant with that might redound to the benefit of labor. And it's this. Capital "quite unintentionally – reduces human labor, expenditure of energy to a minimum. This," he says, "will redound to the benefit of emancipated labor and is the condition of its emancipation." In other words, in Marx's view, the rise of something like automation or artificial intelligence creates conditions and possibilities for the emancipation of labor. In the passage I cited from Marx's pamphlet on the Paris Commune, the issue of the self-emancipation of labor and of the laborer is central. That condition is something which needs to be embraced. But what is it about this condition that makes it so potentially liberatory? The answer is simple. All of this science and technology is increasing the social productivity of labour. One labourer, looking after all of those machines, can produce a vast quantity of commodities in a very short order of time. Here again is Marx in the *Grundrisse*:

To the degree that large industry develops, the creation of real wealth comes to depend less on labour time and on the amount of labour employed than on the power of the agencies set in motion during labour time, whose "powerful effectiveness" is itself in turn out of all proportion to the direct labour time spent on their production, but depends rather on the general state of science and on the progress of technology, or the application of this science to production ... Real wealth manifests itself, rather – and large industry reveals this – in the monstrous disproportion between the labour time applied, and its product.

But then, and here Marx quotes one of the Ricardian socialists writing at that time, "Truly wealthy a nation, when the working day is 6 rather than 12 hours. Wealth is not command over surplus labour time ... but rather disposable time outside that needed in direct production, for every individual and the whole society."

It is this that leads capitalism to produce the possibility for "the free development of individualities" including that of the workers. And by the way, I've said this before but I'm going to say it again. Marx is always, always emphasizing that it's the free development of the individual which is going to be the endpoint of what collective action is going to push for. This common idea that Marx is all about collective action and the suppression of individualism is wrong. It's the other way around. Marx is about mobilizing collective action in order to gain individual liberty. We'll come back to that idea in a moment. But it's the potentiality for the free development of individualities that is the crucial objective here.

All of this is predicated upon "the general reduction of the necessary labor," that is, the amount of labor which is needed to reproduce the daily life of society. The rising productivity of labor will mean that the basic needs of society can be taken care of very easily. This will then allow abundant disposable time for the potential artistic scientific development of the individuals to be set free. At first this will be time for a privileged few but ultimately it will make free disposable time for everyone. That is: setting free individuals to do what they want is critical because you can take care of the basic necessities by use of the sophisticated technology. The problem, says Marx, is that capital itself is a "moving contradiction." It "presses to reduce labor time to a minimum while it posits labor time on the other side as a sole measure and source of wealth." Hence, it diminishes labor time in the necessary form, that is what is really necessary, to increase it in the superfluous form. Now, the superfluous form is what Marx calls surplus value. Who is going to capture the surplus is the question. The problem that Marx identifies is not that the surplus is unavailable but that it is not available to labor. While the tendency "on the one side is to create disposable time," on the other it is "to convert it into surplus labour" for the benefit of the capitalist class. It is not actually being applied to the emancipation of the laborer when it could be. It is being actually applied to the feathering of the nests of the bourgeoisie and therefore the accumulation of wealth through traditional means within the bourgeoisie. So here's the central contradiction. "Truly," Marx says, "the wealth of a nation. How would we understand that? Well," he says, "you can understand it in terms of the mass of money and all the rest of it that somebody commands." But for Marx, "a truly wealthy nation is one in which the working day is six rather than twelve hours. Wealth is not command over surplus labour time but rather disposable time outside that needed in direct production for every individual in the whole society." That is: the wealth of a society is going to be measured by how much disposable free time we all have to do what the hell we like without any constraints because our basic needs are met. And Marx's argument is: you have to have a collective movement to make sure that that kind of society can be constructed. But what gets in the way is, of course, the fact of the dominant class relation and the exercise of capitalist class power.

Now, there's an interesting echo of all of this in our current situation of lockdown and economic collapse as a consequence of the coronavirus. Many of us are in a situation where individually we have a lot of disposable time. Most of us are stuck at home. We can't go to work, we can't do things that we normally do. What are we going to do with our time? If we have kids, of course, then we have quite a bit to do. But we've arrived at this situation in which we have significant disposable time. The second thing is that, of course, we are now experiencing mass unemployment. The last data today suggested that in the United States something like 26 million people have lost their jobs. Now, normally one would say this is a catastrophe and, of course, it is a catastrophe because when you lose your job you lose the capacity to reproduce your own labor power by going to the supermarket because you have no money. Many people have lost their health insurance and many others are having difficulty accessing unemployment benefits. Housing rights are in jeopardy as rents or mortgage payments fall due. Many people in the United States, perhaps as many as 50 percent of the households, have no more than $400 of surplus money in the bank to deal with small emergencies let alone a full-blown crisis of the sort we are now in. These populations are likely to be hitting the streets very soon with starvation staring them and their kids in the face. But look deeper at the situation.

The workforce that is expected to take care of the mounting numbers of the sick and reproducing the minimal services that permit the reproduction of daily life is typically highly gendered, racialized, and ethnicized. This is the "new working class" which is in the forefront of contemporary capitalism and it bears the brunt of either being the workforce most at risk from contracting the virus through their jobs or of being laid off with no resources because of the economic retrenchment enforced by the virus. The contemporary working class in the United States (comprised predominantly of African Americans, Latinx, and waged women) faces the ugly choice of contamination in the name of caring and keeping key features of provision (like grocery stores) open or unemployment with no benefits (such as adequate healthcare). This workforce has long been socialized to behave as good neoliberal subjects (which means blaming themselves or God if anything goes wrong but never daring to suggest capitalism might be the problem). But even good neoliberal subjects can see that there is something wrong with the way this pandemic is being responded to and the disproportionate burden they bear of sustaining the reproduction of the social order.

A collective form of action is required to get us out of this very serious crisis of how to deal with the virus. We need a collective form of action to control its spread: lockdowns and distancing behaviors, all of those kinds of things. This collective action is required to eventually free us up as individuals to live however we like. We cannot do what we like right now. This turns out to be a good metaphor for understanding what capital is about. It is about creating a society where most of us are not free to do what we want because we are actually taken up with producing wealth for the capitalist class. What Marx might say is, well, maybe those 26 million unemployed people, if they could actually find some way of getting enough money to support themselves, buy the commodities they need to survive and rent the house they need to live, then why not pursue mass emancipation from alienating work. In other words, do we want to come out of this crisis by simply saying there's those 26 million people who need to get back to work in some of those pretty awful jobs they may have been involved in before? Is that how we want to come out of it? Or would we want to ask: is there some way to organize the production of basic goods and services so that everybody has something to eat and everybody has a decent place to live and we put a moratorium on any kind of evictions and everybody can live rent free? In other words, isn't this moment where we could actually seriously think about the creation of an alternative society? If we are tough and sophisticated enough to cope with this virus, then why not take on capital at the same time? And instead of saying we all want to go back to work and get those jobs back and restore everything to what it was before this crisis started, maybe we should say why don't we come out of this crisis creating an entirely different kind of social order? Why don't we take that which the current collapsing bourgeois society is pregnant – its astonishing science and technology and productive capacity – and liberate these aspects of artificial intelligence and technological change and organizational forms so that we actually create something radically different than that which existed before? After all, in the midst of this emergency we are already experimenting with all sorts of alternative systems – basic free food supply to poor and impacted neighborhoods and groups, free medical treatments, alternative access structures through the internet, and the like. In fact, the lineaments of a new socialist society are already being laid bare, which is probably why the right-wing and the capitalist class are so anxious to get us back to the status quo ante.

This is a moment of opportunity to think through what an alternative might look like. This is a moment in which the possibility of an alternative actually exists. Instead of just doing a knee jerk reaction and saying, "Oh, we've got to get those 26 million jobs back immediately," no, maybe we should look to expand some of the things that are going on already, such as the collective organization of collective provision. This is already going on in the field of healthcare but it is also beginning to be seen through the socialization of food supply and even cooked meals. In New York City right now several of the restaurant systems have remained open and through donations they're actually providing free meals to the mass of the population that is in that situation, has lost its jobs, that can't move, it can't get around. In other words, instead of saying, well, okay, this is what we do in an emergency, why don't we say, this is the moment when we can start to say to all of those restaurants, okay, your mission is to feed the population so that everybody has a decent meal at least once a day, twice a day. And we have elements of that society already here, which is that, for instance, a lot of schools provide school meals and so on. And so let's keep that going or at least learn the lesson of what might be possible if we cared. Isn't this a moment where we can use this socialist imagination to construct an alternative society? This is not utopian. This is saying, all right, all those restaurants on the Upper West Side which have closed and which are sitting there, kind of dormant. Well, okay. We get the people back in, they start producing the food and they feed the population on the streets and they feed it in the houses and they give it to the old people. We need that collective action in order for all of us to become individually free. In any case, if the 26 million people now unemployed have to go back to work then maybe it should be for 6 rather than 12 hours a day so we can celebrate the rise of a different definition of what it means to live in the wealthiest country in the world. Maybe this is what might make America truly great (leaving the "again" to rot in the dustbin of history).

This is the point that Marx is making again and again and again. That the root of real individualism as opposed to the fake one which is constantly preached in bourgeois ideology, the real root to individual liberty and freedom and emancipation is a situation where all of our needs are taken care of through collective action in such a way as to mean that we only work six hours a day and the rest of the time we do exactly as we please. In other words, isn't this an interesting moment to really think about the dynamism and the possibilities of construction of an alternative socialist society? But in order to get on such an emancipatory path we first have to emancipate ourselves to see that a new imaginary is possible alongside a new reality.

Discussion Questions
and Further Readings

CHAPTER 1: GLOBAL UNREST

- David Harvey, *Brief History of Neoliberalism* (New York: Oxford University Press, 2005).
  - Chapter 1: Freedom's Just Another Word
- David Harvey. *Rebel Cities: From the Right to the City to the Urban Revolution* (London: Verso, 2013).
  - Chapter 5: Reclaiming the City for Anti-Capitalist Struggle
- Karl Marx and V.I. Lenin, *Civil War in France: The Paris Commune* (New York: International Publishers, 1988).

1. What does the current wave of rebellion teach us about the contradictions of capitalism?
2. Why is it critical to understand the problem of compound growth?
3. What kind of path will an anti-capitalist and socialist program need to negotiate in the current crisis?

CHAPTER 2: A BRIEF HISTORY OF NEOLIBERALISM

- David Harvey, *A Brief History of Neoliberalism* (Oxford: Oxford University Press, 2005).
- Lewis F. Powell Jr. to Eugene Sydnor, "Attack on American Free Enterprise System," August 23, 1971, Internet Archive, http://bit.ly/PowellMemo (accessed May 12, 2020).
- Daniel Yergin and Joseph Stanislaw, *The Commanding Heights: The Battle for the World Economy* (New York: Simon & Schuster, 2002).

1. What caused the crash in the financial system in 2007–08?
2. What did Margaret Thatcher mean when she said, "there is no alternative"?
3. Did neoliberalism end in 2007–08?

CHAPTER 3: CONTRADICTIONS OF NEOLIBERALISM

- Karl Marx, *Capital: A Critique of Political Economy, Volume I* (London and New York: Penguin Classics, 1990 [1867]).
  - Chapter 32: Historical Tendency of Capitalist Accumulation
- David Harvey, *A Companion to Marx's Capital, Volume 2* (London and New York: Verso, 2013).
- Jim Mann, *Rise of the Vulcans: The History of Bush's War Cabinet* (New York: Viking, 2004).

1. If capital is compelled to continually diminish wages, then where is the market to come from?
2. Who was blamed for the 2007–08 financial crisis?
3. After the 2007–08 financial crisis, states bailed out the banks and not the people. How was political legitimacy restored in the wake of the crisis?

CHAPTER 4: THE FINANCIALIZATION OF POWER

- David Harvey, *Marx, Capital and the Madness of Economic Reason* (Oxford: Oxford University Press, 2017).

1. What did Goldman Sachs' CEO Lloyd Blankfein mean when he said that Goldman is "doing God's work"?
2. Is finance productive of value?

CHAPTER 5: THE AUTHORITARIAN TURN

- Juan Gabriel Valdés, *Pinochet's Economists: The Chicago School of Economics in Chile* (Cambridge: Cambridge University Press, 1995).
- Jane Mayer, *Dark Money: The Hidden History of the Billionaires Behind the Rise of the Radical Right* (New York: Anchor Books, 2017).

1. Why did the financiers and the Brazilian stock market rally around a neo-fascist like Bolsonaro?
2. What does the emerging alliance between neoliberal economics and right-wing populism look like where you are?

CHAPTER 6: SOCIALISM AND FREEDOM

- Karl Marx, *Capital: A Critique of Political Economy, Volume III* (London and New York: Penguin Classics, 1990 [1894]).
  - Chapter 48: The Trinity Formula
- Karl Marx, *Capita: A Critique of Political Economy, Volume I* (London and New York: Penguin Classics, 1990 [1867]).
  - Chapter Six: The Buying and Selling of Labour-Power
  - Chapter Ten: The Working-Day
- Karl Polanyi, *The Great Transformation: The Political and Economic Origins of Our Time* (Boston: Beacon Press, 2001).
- Naomi Klein, *The Shock Doctrine: The Rise of Disaster Capitalism* (New York: Metropolitan Books/Henry Holt, 2007).

1. Does socialism require a surrender of individual freedom?
2. What did Marx mean when he said, "the realm of freedom begins when the realm of necessity is left behind"?
3. What is the relationship of socialism and free time?

CHAPTER 7: THE SIGNIFICANCE OF CHINA IN THE WORLD ECONOMY

- Xi Jinping, *The Governance of China* (Beijing: Foreign Languages Press, 2014).
- Kai-Fu Lee, *AI Superpowers: China, Silicon Valley, and the New World Order* (Boston: Houghton Mifflin Harcourt, 2018).

1. How did China's resolution to the 2007–08 financial crisis differ from the rest of the world?
2. Is China the future of capitalism or the future of socialism?
3. What could socialism based on artificial intelligence look like?

CHAPTER 8: THE GEOPOLITICS OF CAPITALISM

- David Harvey, *Spaces of Capital: Towards a Critical Geography* (New York: Routledge, 2001).
  - Chapter 14: The Spatial Fix: Hegel, Von Thunen and Marx

- David Harvey, *The New Imperialism* (Oxford and New York: Oxford University Press, 2005).
- Giovanni Arrighi, *The Long Twentieth Century: Money, Power and the Origins of Our Times* (London and New York: Verso, 1994).
- Rosa Luxemburg, *The Accumulation of Capital* (Mansfield Centre, CT: Martino Publishing, 2015 [1913]).

1. What is the relationship of bond-holders to political power?
2. What is the spatial fix?
3. What problem does the spatial fix attempt to solve? Why can it never solve it permanently?

CHAPTER 9: THE GROWTH SYNDROME

- Karl Marx, *Capital: A Critique of Political Economy, Volume I* (London and New York: Penguin Classics, 1990 [1867]).
  - Chapter 14: Division of Labour and Manufacture
  - Chapter 15: Machinery and Modern Industry
- Karl Marx, *Capital: A Critique of Political Economy, Volume III* (London and New York: Penguin Classics, 1990 [1894]).
- Part III: The Law of the Tendency of the Rate of Profit to Fall
  - Chapter 13: The Law as Such
  - Chapter 14: Counteracting Influences
  - Chapter 15: Exposition of the Internal Contradictions of the Law
- Karl Marx, Fred Moseley, ed. *Marx's Economic Manuscript of 1864–1865* (Chicago: Haymarket Books, 2017).
- David Harvey, *Paris, Capital of Modernity* (New York: Routledge, 2006).

1. In much of the Global North, it seems that factories have largely disappeared. What has replaced them?
2. In what sense is the law of the tendency of the rate of profit to fall a double-edged law?
3. How could focusing only on the *rate* of growth and ignoring the *mass* of growth be misleading?

CHAPTER 10: THE EROSION OF CONSUMER CHOICES

- Karl Marx, *Capital: A Critique of Political Economy, Volume I* (London and New York: Penguin Classics, 1990 [1867]).
  - Chapter 15: Machinery and Modern Industry
- David Harvey, *Rebel Cities: From the Right to the City to the Urban Revolution* (London: Verso, 2013).
- André Gorz, *Critique of Economic Reason* (London, Verso, 1989).

1. How autonomous are we in terms of our consumer choices?
2. What drives urban development today?
3. To what degree is extractivism necessary for the reproduction of contemporary ways of life?

CHAPTER 11: PRIMITIVE OR ORIGINAL ACCUMULATION

- Rosa Luxemburg, *The Accumulation of Capital* (Mansfield Centre, CT: Martino Publishing, 2015 [1913]).
- Karl Marx, *Capital: A Critique of Political Economy, Volume I* (New York: Penguin Books, 1990).
  - Chapter 26: The Secret of Primitive Accumulation
  - Chapter 27: The Expropriation of the Agricultural Population from the Land
  - Chapter 28: Bloody Legislation Against the Expropriated since the End of the Fifteenth Century. The Forcing Down of Wages by Act of Parliament
  - Chapter 29: The Genesis of the Capitalist Farmer
  - Chapter 30: Impact of the Agricultural Revolution on Industry The Creation of a Home Market for Industrial Capital
  - Chapter 31: The Genesis of the Industrial Capitalist
  - Chapter 32: The Historical Tendency of Capitalist Accumulation
  - Chapter 33: The Modern Theory of Colonization
- Michael Perelman, *The Invention of Capitalism: Classical Political Economy and the Secret History of Primitive Accumulation* (Durham, NC: Duke University Press, 2000).
- Hannah Arendt, *Imperialism* (New York: Harcourt Brace, 1968).

1. What were the main purposes of so-called "primitive accumulation"?
2. To what degree are the processes of primitive accumulation that Marx described still with us?

CHAPTER 12: ACCUMULATION BY DISPOSSESSION

- David Harvey, *The New Imperialism* (Oxford: Oxford University Press, 2003).
  - Chapter 4: Accumulation by Dispossession

1. What is the difference between "primitive accumulation" and "accumulation by dispossession"?
2. What are examples of struggles against accumulation by dispossession?

CHAPTER 13: PRODUCTION AND REALIZATION

- Karl Marx, *The Marx-Engels Reader*, second edition, ed. Robert C. Tucker (New York: W.W. Norton, 1978).
- "The Coming Upheaval," pp. 218–19, the concluding passage from Karl Marx, 1847, *The Poverty of Philosophy*.
- Karl Marx, *Grundrisse: Foundations of the Critique of Political Economy* (New York: Penguin Books, 1993).
- Silvia Federici, *Caliban and the Witch: Women, the Body, and Primitive Accumulation* (New York: Autonomedia, 2004).
- "Raise Up for $15, Fight for $15," https://fightfor15.org/raiseup/ (accessed May 12, 2020).

1. Why is it important to understand what Marx called a "class-in-itself" versus a "class-for-itself"?
2. Is transportation productive of value?
3. What does the impact of the closures due to the coronavirus tell you about the constitution of the present working class where you live?

CHAPTER 14: CARBON DIOXIDE EMISSIONS AND CLIMATE CHANGE

- David Harvey, *Justice, Nature, and the Geography of Difference* (Cambridge, MA: Blackwell, 1996).

1. Where did the increase in mass of carbon dioxide in the atmosphere come from?
2. How can activists work to take carbon dioxide out of the atmosphere and put it back underground?

CHAPTER 15: RATE VERSUS MASS OF SURPLUS VALUE

- Karl Marx, *Capital: A Critique of Political Economy, Volume I* (New York: Penguin Books, 1990).
  - Chapter 1: The Commodity
  - Chapter 10: The Working-Day
  - Chapter 11: The Rate and Mass of Surplus-Value
- Karl Marx, *Capital: A Critique of Political Economy, Volume III* (New York: Penguin Books, 1991).
  - Part III: The Law of the Tendential Fall in the Rate of Profit
  - Chapter 13: The Law Itself
  - Chapter 14: Counteracting Influences
  - Chapter 15: Development of the Law's Internal Contradictions
- Paul Sweezy and Paul A. Baran, *Monopoly Capital: An Essay on the American Economic and Social Order* (New York: Monthly Review Press, 1966).
- Michael Roberts Blog, https://thenextrecession.wordpress.com (accessed May 12, 2020).

1. Are capitalists more concerned about the mass of surplus value that they get or the rate at which they're getting it?
2. What is Marx's argument about the equalization of the rate of profit?
3. How does Marx's argument help us understand the period of globalization since the 1980s?

CHAPTER 16: ALIENATION

- Karl Marx, *Economic and Philosophical Manuscripts of 1844* (Moscow: Progress Publishers, 1959).
- Karl Marx, *Grundrisse: Foundations of the Critique of Political Economy* (New York: Penguin Books, 1993).

- Karl Marx, *Capital: A Critique of Political Economy, Volume I* (New York: Penguin Books, 1990).
  - Chapter 10: The Working-Day
- Émile Zola, *Au Bonheur des Dames (The Ladies' Delight)* (New York: Penguin Books, 2001).

1. How did Marx define the concept of alienation?
2. How can Marx's theory of alienation help us understand contemporary conditions of labor?

CHAPTER 17: ALIENATION AT WORK: THE POLITICS OF A PLANT CLOSURE

- Paul Sweezy and Paul A. Baran, *Monopoly Capital: An Essay on the American Economic and Social Order* (New York: Monthly Review Press, 1966).
- LaToya Ruby Frazier: The Last Cruze, http://bit.ly/LastCruze (accessed May 12, 2020).

1. What does LaToya Ruby Frazier's photo essay teach us about the impact of the General Motors plant closure on workers, families, and children?
2. Why are the auto companies in Detroit good examples of how monopoly capitalism worked?
3. How has globalization changed the way capital views labor?

CHAPTER 18: ANTI-CAPITALIST POLITICS IN THE TIME OF COVID-19

- Karl Marx, *Grundrisse: Foundations of the Critique of Political Economy* (New York: Penguin Books, 1993).

1. How might the dominant neoliberal economic model, with its sagging legitimacy and delicate health, absorb and survive the inevitable impacts of a pandemic?
2. How should we evaluate the convenient myth that infectious diseases do not acknowledge class or other social barriers and boundaries?

CHAPTER 19: THE COLLECTIVE RESPONSE
TO A COLLECTIVE DILEMMA

- Karl Marx, *Grundrisse: Foundations of the Critique of Political Economy* (New York: Penguin Books, 1993), pp. 650–710.
- Karl Marx and V.I. Lenin, *Civil War in France: The Paris Commune* (New York, International Publishers, 1988).
1. How does the mobilization of science and technology as forms of knowledge affect the way that labor is incorporated into production processes within capitalism?
2. What is Marx's argument about the self-emancipation of labor?
3. How might activists view the current crisis as an opportunity to envision an alternative socialist society?

Index

Thanks to our Patreon Subscribers:

Abdul Alkalimat
Andrew Perry

Who have shown their generosity and comradeship in difficult times.

Check out the other perks you get by subscribing to our Patreon – visit patreon.com/plutopress.

Subscriptions start from £3 a month.